The ENEMIES *of*
CHRISTOPHER
COLUMBUS

Thomas A. Bowden is an attorney in private practice in Baltimore, Maryland. A graduate of the University of Maryland School of Law, he also holds degrees in American history from the University of Kentucky and the University of Delaware. As a Senior Writer for the Ayn Rand Institute, he has applied Ayn Rand's philosophy of Objectivism to current events in a variety of widely published op-eds and in numerous radio and television appearances. His live and taped lecture courses on American legal history and jurisprudence have attracted an international audience.

The ENEMIES *of* CHRISTOPHER COLUMBUS

Answers to Critical Questions
About the Spread
of Western Civilization

Revised Edition

By Thomas A. Bowden

Published by:
The Paper Tiger, Inc.
722 Upper Cherrytown Road
Kerhonkson, NY 12446-1331

www.papertig.com

ISBN: 1-889439-36-3

Cover image © Bettmann/CORBIS

To Susan and John — and to Haxta

Throughout the centuries there were men who took first steps down new roads armed with nothing but their own vision. Their goals differed, but they all had this in common: that the step was first, the road new, the vision unborrowed, and the response they received—hatred.

—Ayn Rand,
The Fountainhead

CONTENTS

Appendices

Commentary

Q

Who are the enemies of
Christopher Columbus – and
why do they seek to destroy
his reputation?

A

Traditionally, Columbus's epic voyage of 1492 was taught as the first chapter of a glorious story: the discovery and settlement of North America, culminating in the birth and explosive growth of a new and independent nation, the United States of America. Columbus himself was viewed as an heroic character who braved the unknown in search of a western trade route to the Indies and ended up discovering the New World.

In recent years, however, the enemies of Christopher Columbus have succeeded in damaging, if not demolishing, his historical reputation. Today, Columbus is seen not as a hero but as an inept sailor turned brutal conqueror, and his voyage is taught as the opening assault in a genocidal campaign by cruel imperialists bent on exterminating the peaceful natives, who inhabited an idyllic wilderness in harmony with the environment.

Who are these enemies of Christopher Columbus? They include:

- *Religious leaders* such as those who, on the five hundredth anniversary of Columbus's voyage, declared that 1992 should be a "year of reflection and repentance," not celebration, because Columbus inaugurated an era of "invasion, genocide, slavery, 'ecocide,' and exploitation of the wealth of the land." *(National Council of Churches of Christ in the USA).*

- *Teachers* such as those who urge that Columbus be presented in a more "realistic light" by stressing the negative consequences of colonialism (including disease, slavery, and slaughter) and describing Columbus's voyage "without saying [whether] he is a hero or not." *(American Historical Association; National Associations of Elementary School Principals and of Secondary School Principals).*

- *Indians* such as those who charge that Columbus initiated a "five-century feeding frenzy that has left Native people and this red quarter of Mother Earth in a state of emergency" and who call on fellow Indians to reject the idea that "genocide and ecocide are offset by the benefits of horses, cut-glass beads, pickup trucks and microwave ovens." *(Suzan Shown Harjo).*

- *Activists* such as those who declare that "Columbus was the beginning of the American holocaust, ethnic cleansing characterized by murder, torture, raping, pillaging, robbery, slavery, kidnapping, and forced removals of Indian people from their homelands" *(American Indian Movement)* and the noted actor who demanded that his name be removed from the credits of a movie in which he appeared because it failed to portray Columbus as "the true villain he was." *(Marlon Brando;* Christopher Columbus: The Discovery).

- *Demonstrators* such as those who march and carry signs saying: "Columbus murdered a continent" and pour fake blood on public statutes of Columbus.
- *Authors and intellectuals* such as those who wrote that Columbus "opened the Atlantic slave trade and launched one of the greatest waves of genocide known in history" *(Jack Weatherford)* and that Columbus "inaugurated the greatest experiment in political, economic, and cultural cannibalism in the history of the Western world." *(Stephen Greenblatt)*
- *Politicians* such as those in Berkeley, California, who replaced Columbus Day with "Indigenous Peoples Day" to celebrate the aborigines' "sustainable peaceful culture based on cooperation among neighbors, on respect for the land and for all creatures living on it," a culture that was "disrupted and destroyed" by the arrival of Europeans.

That Columbus is held in contempt by many modern opinion leaders is beyond doubt. But what also becomes clear upon further study is that the *ideas* underlying these attacks are destroying not only the reputation of Columbus but that of the civilization he brought with him—the civilization that was in the midst of a great Renaissance in 1492—the civilization that eventually spawned the Enlightenment, the Industrial Revolution, and the United States of America, the first nation in history founded on the principle of individual rights—the civilization that has demonstrated to every honest observer the power of the human mind to generate wealth and happiness on an unprecedented scale.

The real victim of the incessant attacks on Christopher Columbus is Western civilization itself.

To destroy the good reputation of an entire civilization is a formidable task; it requires, among many other things, wholesale changes in the way history is taught to new generations. On the defensive in this battle are those who explain historical events from the perspective of Western civilization.[1] Such teachers act, implicitly or explicitly, on the premise that Western civilization, which stands for reason, science, individualism, and progress, is objectively superior to all other cultures that the world has known, *because* it gives rise to all the values on which man's life demonstrably depends.

The opposite view is cultural relativism, which holds that there is no standard by which to judge one culture, or one cultural value, superior to another. On this view (which is "politically correct" and rarely questioned today), there are no moral absolutes, and therefore no good reason to value Western civilization (including modern America) over primitive Indian savagery. If we think our culture is superior, it is only because we are "conditioned" to think that way by our membership in that very culture.

Cultural relativism, as Michael Berliner has explained, is invalid because it is self-contradictory:

> [Relativism] is a self-refuting doctrine, for it claims objective validity for itself, when it's advocating the impossibility of objective validity; it steps outside a culture to claim that one cannot step outside a culture; it condemns as immoral the whole institution of condemnation and praise.

Such logical refutation, however, has no impact on the adherents of cultural relativism, because logic itself is, to them, a subjective preference without universal application.

In recent years, cultural relativism has morphed into *multiculturalism,* which cashes in on this evaluative emasculation by

---

1. This perspective is sometimes called "Eurocentric," which is a misnomer because it implies a racial basis for emphasizing the achievements of Western civilization. In fact, reason knows no race, and the only valid reason for teaching history from the perspective of Western civilization lies in the objective merits and achievements of that civilization, compared to all others.

proclaiming, in effect, as follows: Since no culture can be proven superior to any other, it is inexcusably arrogant for educators to go on inculcating in their students the values of Western civilization—or any other value system, for that matter. Indeed, why should young people even attempt the quixotic task of selecting the "right" values on logical or historical grounds from among dozens of discredited, outmoded options? Far better for students to accept automatic membership in one or more social groups, defined by *unchosen* physical or ethnic attributes: skin color, ancestry, race, language, birthplace, gender. In this way, the multicultural argument turns its back on Western civilization and calls for a return to primitive tribalism.

On reading these words, most Americans will be reluctant to believe that any modern ideology could actually seek to abandon civilization and embrace the life of a savage. The chief purpose of this book is to warn that the enemies of Christopher Columbus are serious, and that the ideas they endorse, if not refuted and rejected, will end in the death of science, the destruction of the cities, and the impoverishment of the human race.

There is a concept in philosophy that describes the mental state of people who crave destruction for the sake of destruction, who want to tear down civilization for the thrill of watching it fall. The concept is *nihilism,* and as Peter Schwartz has shown at length elsewhere, it applies to the whole multicultural movement:

> [The multiculturalists] argue, not for the obvious proposition that many cultures exist, but for the invidious proposition that all are equal in value. Every culture is "different," they say—but none is superior. And what is the ultimate goal of this ideology? To *reverse* the process of civilization, by wrenching man back to a primeval state of existence.

One who seeks historical examples of a primeval state of existence need look no further than pre-Columbian America. This accounts for the multiculturalists' overweening interest in the Indian lifestyle—

and for the implacable hostility they display toward the memory of Christopher Columbus.

Thus, the debate over Columbus is much wider than the question of whether he or his followers mistreated some Indians. The fundamental issue is whether the settlement of America by the bearers of Western civilization over the past five centuries was good or evil. Those who regard that process as evil want Columbus to bear blame for starting it all, and they use him as a symbol of everything they hate about the West, so as to strangle any sense of pride in the spread of civilization to the New World. "Those who ultimately advocate and defend the realities of European culture and its industrialism are my enemies," says Indian activist Russell Means, a noted critic of Columbus.

The two sides of this conflict are sharply drawn: One holds that Western civilization is objectively superior and worth defending to the death, while the other holds that Western civilization is evil and must be destroyed. Now, at the dawn of the twenty-first century, with Western civilization under martial attack by militant Islamic fundamentalists, it is more important than ever to choose sides. As President Bush said to the nations of the world at the start of America's war against terrorism, "You're either with us or against us." Those who would defend and uphold the values of Western civilization must be willing to make the same bold declaration to the enemies of Christopher Columbus.

Q

But isn't it true that no one culture is superior to another? What's right for one is not necessarily right for the other. It's all subjective. So, isn't multiculturalism the proper approach?

A

Judging the merits of a civilization is an objective, rational inquiry, not just an expression of one's subjective preference based on place of birth, race, or ethnicity. Contrary to the tenets of multiculturalism, it is not only possible but vitally necessary to judge societies according to how well civilized they are.

Civilization is the historical process by which human beings apply *reason* to all aspects of their lives: philosophy, morality, politics, economic production, social relations, the humanities, and the arts. Civilization makes human existence safe, prosperous, and enjoyable.

Animals, whose behavior is governed by instinct, cannot civilize themselves. But human beings have the power of conceptual thought, which includes the ability to preserve in language the results of their thinking, so that every achievement of the reasoning mind—in agriculture, science, medicine, technology, commerce, law, art, and a thousand other subjects—can be handed down to the next generation, to be built upon and improved, then handed down again, in a never-ending march of progress.

The more consistent a society's commitment to reason, the more dynamic the resulting civilization, and the more likely it is to display the hallmarks of the great historical civilizations, such as ancient Greece, Rome, and the United States of America. These hallmarks include large cities, growing populations, the division of labor, improving standards of living, longer life expectancy, widening political freedom, the growth of leisure, refined manners, and an emerging respect for the individual.

Is there an objective standard by which to judge whether such progress is good or bad? Ayn Rand said yes, there is such a standard, but it is not to be found in mystic revelations from God or in one's subjective preference for the society into which one was born. Rather, the standard inheres in man's nature as a living being who, like any other living thing, will die unless he acts for his own survival in accordance with his nature. "An organism's life," Ayn Rand said, "is its *standard of value:* that which furthers its life is the *good,* that which threatens it is the *evil.*" Because reason is man's means of survival, she defined man's particular standard of value as "the terms, methods, conditions and goals required for the survival of a rational being through the whole of his lifespan—in all those aspects of existence which are open to his choice." If such is the objective standard by which human actions should be judged, whether alone or in society, then it follows that the most rational civilization—the one that embodies the end product of man's best thinking and action since the beginning of time—represents the highest social value possible to mankind, and an enormous *good*.

Western civilization is that most rational civilization, that highest social value.

Underlying every achievement of Western civilization has been a restless intellectual ambition, a striving for depth and breadth of knowledge, all aimed at understanding the world and how best to live in it, and all made possible by a scientific view of the universe. This zeal for understanding, this desire on the part of civilized man to *use* his rational faculty, gives him the power to see a cloth fluttering in the wind and conceive of a sail—to observe a floating lodestone and conceive of a compass—to see a ship vanishing gradually over the horizon and conceive of the earth as a globe—to visualize that globe and measure its size—to take that measurement and plan a voyage of discovery—to make that voyage and then retrace one's path—to see coastlines along the way and conceive of continents and islands—to make maps showing all that—and to use the products of these adventures to meet still greater challenges, moving mankind forward into a beckoning future. As in geographical exploration, so in every realm of human existence, civilization expands the reach of human understanding into every niche of the universe, in search of all that might serve human life.

Contrast this breadth of intellectual endeavor with the constricted mental outlook of the savage, whose world view is dominated by animism, the primitive notion that everything in the universe is inhabited by powerful spirits whose nature remains mysterious.[2] The

---

2. The essence of animism was perhaps best captured by Jaime de Angulo, an anthropologist who lived with the Pit River Indians of northern California. These Indians believed that "the essence of religion is 'the spirit of wonder,' the recognition of power as a mysterious concentrated form of nonmaterial energy, of something loose in the world and

(continued...)

anxiety that necessarily results from such superstition induces cognitive paralysis, discouraging the uncivilized man from expanding his knowledge of the world. It is the savage's lot to see one of his tribe's crude boats vanishing gradually over the horizon and feel dread that the water spirits might prevent its return—to take that dread and turn it into a frenzied dance of supplication—to take that dance and make it into a ritual, to be repeated generation after generation—to invent a new ritual for every danger, for every wild animal, flood, famine, drought, or illness that threatens his marginal existence—and finally, to have nothing to pass on to the next generation but a pile of arrowheads, some animal skins, and a vision of the future that differs not from the past. Immobilized by superstition, the savage society is helpless before the forces of nature, and consequently its members cannot control the course of their own lives.

The point is this simple: It is better to be rich, healthy, and safe than to be poor, sick, and afraid. These are the two extremes on the spectrum. The importance of being at one end rather than the other is not simply a matter of subjective preference. It is the difference between life—*man's* life—and squalid death. People who fail to civilize themselves are doomed to live in filth, hunger, and fear—and to die before their time.

For these reasons, multiculturalism is wrong. Not all societies are equal; some have implemented reason more thoroughly than others. It is not any "cultural conditioning" that makes us believe, for instance, that telephoning from an air-conditioned apartment for pizza delivery is preferable to gnawing on vermin-ridden meat in a sweltering tepee—or that luxury cruise ships are preferable to

---

(...continued)

contained in a more or less condensed degree by every object." Consistent with this state of mind, the Mayas believed the stones of their temples to be inhabited by spirits. Thus they could never bring themselves to tear down a crumbling building, for fear of insulting the spirits. Instead, they built new buildings around the old, like layers of an onion.

dugout canoes—or that laser surgery is preferable to a shaman's spells.[3]

No one who cares about his own life, or those of his loved ones, can afford to engage in the incredible pretense of multiculturalism.

---

3.   Incidentally, only Western civilization is sophisticated enough to have originated the idea that it is inferior. Primitive societies are uniformly ethnocentric, viewing social reality, in effect, as "us versus everyone else." Such a mentality does not permit the emergence of tribal self-hatred, since that would spell instant destruction at the hands of other tribes. In this limited sense, the pre-Columbian Indians were arguably superior to modern academics who damn America and its achievements, out of guilt or a desire to appease.

Q

Accepting man's life as an objective standard by which cultures can be compared, how do Western and Indian societies stack up against each other?

A

If we evaluate Western civilization and Indian societies by the standard of man's life, the conclusion is inescapable: Western civilization is superior.

The essential achievement of Western civilization—the product of centuries of individual efforts, from classical Greece through the Renaissance and the Industrial Revolution to the present—has been to establish, and implement in practice, the following truths:

1. The universe operates according to natural law rather than being controlled by supernatural powers or mysterious spirits;

2. By observing nature and applying reason, through the scientific method, men can understand the natural laws by which

things work and apply that understanding to the task of living on earth;

3. By assuming self-responsibility, each individual can shape the course of his own life rather than being controlled by the will of the tribe;

4. By choosing to work hard, men can achieve a constantly improving standard of living through production, invention, technology, trade, and the accumulation and transfer of knowledge from generation to generation;

5. Governments that protect the rights to life, liberty, property, and the pursuit of happiness establish spheres of freedom within which individuals can achieve the best that is possible to them;

6. Artists, by studying reality and the methods by which human beings perceive it, can provide vital inspiration by re-creating reality in an idealized form.

Adherents of these Western values have applied reason more thoroughly, to more aspects of life on earth, than have the adherents of any other culture. In America, long a haven for the best elements of Western civilization, the results are all around us—in the buildings and highways that grace our cities, in the grocery stores that supply our food, in the spaceships that extend our reach to distant planets, in the profusion of books and art works and leisure time activities that combine with numerous other achievements to afford each individual's life a limitless horizon. Wherever Western civilization dominates, human life flourishes.

Now consider pre-Columbian Indian life. Let us leave aside for the moment the relatively advanced cultures of the Aztecs, Incas, and Mayas, and focus on the nomadic and village-dwelling Indians of North America. Not having developed an Aristotle of their own, these Indians had neither discovered the laws of logic nor formed a concept of natural law. Instead, they believed the universe to be ruled by fickle, inscrutable spirits that require unflinching obedience to deliberately mind-numbing rituals and taboos. Lacking an appreciation of reason and causality, they had developed no science or mathematics. The sanctity of individual life held no place in their thinking; rather, they thought in terms of kinship group or tribe, and the life of each individual was justified by its contribution to some such collective. Politically, Indians never developed the idea of individual rights. Warfare between tribes was widespread and brutally destructive. Within tribes, each individual was required to follow tribal customs and taboos. Virtually all these Indians were either hunters, gatherers, fishers, or planters; progress from generation to generation was minimal. These Indians were still mired in the stone age. They were miserably poor, not only by today's standards but by those of fifteenth century Europe. All Indians—chiefs as well as warriors, shamans as well as women—were subject to a variety of economic and physical catastrophes (such as floods, famines, pestilence, and epidemic disease) that modern societies have tamed or forgotten.

Turning now to the more advanced cultures of Mexico and Peru, we see that they also shared most of these primitive characteristics, including superstition and the tribal mentality. These societies did engage in agriculture, eking out enough surplus food to support the beginnings of a division of labor. This in turn made it possible to undertake labor-intensive projects such as roads, causeways, temples, and pyramids. These were important signs of genuine progress. However, even the priests and ruling classes in these societies had no concept of reason or its role in human life. Because they lacked the intellectual tools to be self-critical, they behaved irrationally, using their wealth and power to conquer weaker tribes, extort tribute, capture slaves, and slaughter sacrificial victims.

None of this implies moral failure or racial inferiority on the part of the pre-Columbian Indians; rather, they simply had not yet achieved what the Europeans had. On the other hand, the coming of the Europeans meant there was no need to wait millennia for some ingenious Indian to figure out how to build a wheeled cart, or to discover the laws of logic. So it was with thousands of other accomplishments, large and small, that Indians could have eventually reached on their own but were now able to receive from the Europeans. For this reason alone, it is gratitude and not hostility that Christopher Columbus deserves from the descendants of the American aborigines.

To appreciate the value of Western civilization is not to claim that every intellectual, scientific, and technological development originated in the West. There are many examples—such as the compass, which came from the Chinese by way of the Arabs—of the creativity of other cultures. "Just as there is no such thing as a collective or racial mind," Ayn Rand has written, "so there is no such thing as a collective or racial achievement. . . . A genius is a genius, regardless of the number of morons who belong to the same race—and a moron is a moron, regardless of the number of geniuses who share his racial origin." Western civilization, to the extent that reason reigns supreme, recognizes the merit in the objective achievements of individuals of any race in any culture, and adopts from each that which truly serves human needs.

When the differences between Western civilization and Indian society are brought into full focus, the relative merits of the two become clear. We who are fortunate enough to live in the twenty-first century can have no excuse for valuing any primitive culture over Western civilization—not if our standard of choice is that which is best for human life. Western civilization, as relatively advanced as it was in 1492, had not fully developed its present contours; much was then mere potential. Even in later years, the civilizing process was gradual, progressing in fits and starts and consuming many centuries. But today, men and women of all races, ages, religions, and ethnic backgrounds should admire the achievements of Western civilization, which far surpass those of any other culture, especially that of the prehistoric Indians. Here at the dawn of the twenty-first century, Western civilization is truly the hope of the world, for the descendants of Indians as well as the descendants of Europeans.

Q

Even if Western civilization is superior to Indian savagery, does that necessarily imply that Europeans had a right to displace the Indians?

A

Savagery and civilization cannot co-exist in the same geographical area. Civilized people must be able to depend on their neighbors to understand and obey the principles of individual rights as expressed in written laws that define land boundaries, enforce contracts, and protect personal property. Primitive peoples, who have not yet reached the concept of a universal moral law governing all human beings as individuals, cannot act on such principles or be relied upon to obey such laws. Lacking the ability to rule their lives by reason, savages inevitably succumb to a whole range of non-rational influences—such as fear, superstition, drug-induced hallucinations, hatred of outsiders, revenge, or lust for conquest—that propel them onto the warpath at unpredictable intervals. The Europeans, in establishing their settlements in the New World, found themselves enmeshed in precisely this conflict between civilization and barbarism. Hence they confronted a fundamental choice: to marshal their superior powers and displace the Indians, or else turn around and sail home.

In that context, the European immigrants had an absolute right to settle America and displace the Indians—by force when necessary. However, to the extent that individual Indians (such as Pocahontas, who married an Englishman) were capable of grasping and abiding by the principles of civilized behavior, they should have been permitted and encouraged to become full citizens with full rights. Of course, the choice to assimilate oneself into Western society is viewed by multiculturalists as a betrayal of ethnic identity, and hence statistics on assimilation are not well publicized.

By what moral standard could the geographical spread of Western civilization be criticized? Certainly not by any standard held by the Indians, from whose perspective the Europeans did nothing wrong. The Indians had not conceived any moral standard by which the victory of one tribe over another could be judged good or bad; rather, each tribe was a law unto itself, with brute strength the ultimate arbiter. By this muscle-power standard, the Europeans were simply a stronger tribe that could not be defeated.

The contemporary enemies of Christopher Columbus, on the other hand, borrow civilization's *own* standards of decency and fair treatment in an attempt to blacken the reputation of civilization itself, its standards, and everything to which it leads. While ignoring the long record of brutal conflict between and among Indians, these critics seize upon particular instances of European mistreatment of Indians as evidence that Western civilization itself should be condemned. But any such instances as might be proven (which primarily involve the activities of Spaniards in Latin America) establish at most that certain Europeans *abandoned* civilized standards in victimizing the Indians. The problem in such cases was not too much civilization, but too little. The modern enemies of Christopher Columbus would be more honest if they stated openly that America is evil because it replaced wild buffalo herds with hamburger stands, tepees with tract houses, and shamans with brain surgeons.

For millennia, the American Indians' marginal existence had been plagued by bloody wars and senseless torture, with no end in sight. Then came Columbus and the other Europeans, who brought with them not just military prowess but something of far greater value, to enrich the lives of both victor and vanquished. They brought great *ideas:* the idea of natural law, to replace animism—reason, to replace superstition—self-interest, to replace self-sacrifice—individual freedom, to replace tribal collectivism—civility, to replace barbarism. In a spectacularly short time, Western civilization would show the world how to establish a society based on individual rights, including especially the private ownership of property, a society in which people dealt with each other not by force of arms but by appeals to the mind, through persuasion. It is only by comparison with this civilized system that the bloody tactics of American Indians, as well as some sixteenth century Europeans, seem primitive. Let us not revile the culture that brought us to this glorious day.

Q

Of what importance to us, in the present, is the history of men long dead, such as Christopher Columbus? What difference does it make whether or not we accurately understand the Columbus story?

A

The study of history originates in our need to evaluate the ideas and characters of the *living* people around us, in order to assess their potential for good or evil in relation to our own lives. Philosophers and social scientists draw upon historical data in formulating and verifying the principles that guide our most important decisions. This is especially true with regard to complex social issues, such as the efficacy of different social systems, the character of different nations, and the value of different cultures.

It is not enough to look around and see cars, hospitals, and grocery stores and conclude that societies with such wealth are superior to those that lack it. We need to know *how the goods got here*, i.e., what ideas and values led to their creation by what people? Such causal investigation is not easy. The creation of wealth and the other products of civilization occurs on such a grand scale, geographically and chronologically, that it is impossible for any one individual to grasp the process from personal observation. For example, one could not fully understand the global importance of the scientific method in promoting human health and happiness simply by extrapolating from one's personal experience (even if one's job was that of a laboratory scientist). One needs to understand how Copernicus led to Galileo, who led to Newton, who led to Einstein, who led to the discovery of atomic energy. Hence, the discipline of history arises, for the purpose of investigating the evidence pertaining to important past events and then explaining their causes. Only through history can we fully grasp the long-term effects of ideas in practice. We apply this knowledge when assessing the ideas and values of those around us, in the present. This is why it is essential for history teachers to trace cause and effect accurately.

In short, we study the dead in order to judge the living.

Thus when an historian errs, he damages not merely the historical reputations of dead people but also the reputation of every living person who embraces the same ideas that the dead people practiced. For example, if the life story of Christopher Columbus is twisted, so as to make it appear that the choice to expand one's knowledge of the world in pursuit of personal goals leads men to become arrogant and contemptuous of human life, creating a bloody trail of plunder, conquest, and "ecocide," it is not Columbus who suffers—he is beyond suffering. Rather, those who suffer are all the *living* persons who act on the premise that expanding their knowledge of the world in pursuit of their self-interest promotes human life rather than destroying it. It is *their* reputations that now become suspect, in the eyes of every person who is ignorant of the true history of Western civilization.

By the same token, faulty analysis of cause and effect can enhance the reputation of living persons who don't deserve it. As an example, suppose that students come away from their study of Columbus with the erroneous idea that pre-Columbian Indians—who never developed a concept of natural law and spent much of their time trying to appease imaginary gods through bizarre rituals and bloody sacrifices—actually lived happier, cleaner, and safer lives than modern-day people who manipulate nature for their own ends by means of science and industry. The pre-Columbian Indians themselves cannot benefit from this error—they are long dead. Who does benefit? Those *living* Indians (and their non-Indian brothers in spirit) who want to act *now* on the premise that senseless ritual and self-sacrifice promote human life rather than destroying it. It is *their* reputations that now acquire a new, undeserved luster in the eyes of every person who is ignorant of the true history of Western civilization.

Only such historical inversion can account for travesties like the article in *Parade* magazine, a popular Sunday newspaper supplement, that appeared the day before Columbus Day, 1992. In that article, entitled "We Are All Related," the author laments the "500 years of loss and suffering" that followed Columbus's first voyage. The article then urges Americans to adopt such "profound tenets" of Indian life as "The dream world is the real world" and "we belong to the earth, and we have a sacred duty to protect it and return thanks for the gifts of life."

There is no option here to do without a thorough grounding in the history of Western civilization. The need for historical proof is just one instance of our need to connect *all* of our thoughts to reality, by means of recalling past observations. Because the essence of Western civilization is a body of knowledge, a series of principles concerning the relationship between man and reality, historical evidence is crucial, as proof of those ideas' continuing effects *in the future.*

Contrary to the perceptions of many people, therefore, the purpose of teaching history is not to torture students with piles of random facts, connected by nothing and leading nowhere. Rather, accurate historical instruction displays the highest respect for students' minds. By teaching history, each generation declares to the next, in effect: Don't take our values on faith—look at the objective historical evidence that supports them, and judge for yourselves.

Q

Why should the history of Western civilization dominate the classroom, at the expense of Indian history? Since history is the record of everything that happened in mankind's past, doesn't each historical society merit "equal time"?

A

History, properly taught, is not simply the record of everything that happened in the past, assembled and spewed forth willy-nilly. Selectivity is essential in teaching history, as in teaching any other subject. Even if there were unlimited time to learn "everything that happened," such an approach would not address the needs of a conceptual consciousness, which must focus on *essentials*.

How, then, should history teachers decide which events to teach and which to omit? By gauging the importance of the general truths to be validated by the historical truths being taught.

By way of analogy, suppose one had to choose between hearing the life story of some homeless drifter and learning the important childhood events of one's future husband or wife. The obviously better choice is the latter, because it is more important to form generalizations about the character of one's future spouse than about that of a stranger. By the same token, it is entirely proper to give little or no attention to Indian history while stressing the history of Western civilization. Why? Because it is objectively more important to understand why and how Western civilization *promotes* human life than to understand why and how Indian culture is *powerless* to promote human life.

For example, the student who understands, from a study of Western civilization, that the scientific method yields an enormous range of scientific and technological achievements, will be equipped to argue intelligently for social policies that provide the freedom necessary for scientific endeavors. This is a major priority. If he has any time left over, he may benefit from observing that rain dances and human sacrifices in pre-Columbian Indian societies achieved nothing but the waste of human life. The value of that history is chiefly to confirm one's conclusions about the essential tenets of Western civilization, by providing negative contrast.

If it were otherwise, history would properly be written from a different perspective. For example, if it were really true that supernatural forces would make the sun disappear unless we supplied fresh human blood to fuel its daily trek across the sky, as the Aztecs believed, and if the Aztecs had really found the secret to pleasing these gods, then we would need to de-emphasize the history of Western civilization and stress the history of the Aztecs, so that we might understand the historical evidence in support of human sacrifice. Merely to give this example, however, is to expose the preposterousness of suggesting that Indian societies merit equal or greater attention.

One who has fully grasped the history of Western civilization is not likely to be fooled by those who contend that Indian culture is superior. But one who studies only primitive cultures will never glimpse the pinnacle of Western civilization or understand its value.

The hierarchical choices facing teachers of history are quite complex, and many options exist regarding emphasis. But how could there be any reasonable disagreement over the need to understand the history of Western civilization above all others? We are not operating in an historical vacuum. It is not as if we are starting at the beginning of historical time, surrounded by a dozen primitive societies, none of them advanced beyond the rest, and trying to decide on the basis of scanty evidence which to study. Rather, we have the benefit of mountains of historical research summarizing the experience of millions of people over thousands of years, leading ineluctably to the conclusion that Western civilization is superior in every essential respect.

It remains only for the teachers to teach it.

Q

Why is it proper to teach that Columbus "discovered" America, when in fact there were many people already here when Columbus landed?

A

What makes a person's life historically significant is its influence on human progress, for good or ill. Thus, a person should not be judged historically by what he inherits from his surrounding culture, but rather by what he adds to, or detracts from, that culture. For example, Thomas Jefferson's historical significance lies not in his ownership of slaves but in his role in founding the United States of America, especially his authorship of the Declaration of Independence, which crystallized the moral and political ideals of a nation and pointed the way toward a society of rational self-interest in which all people, including the slaves, would soon be free. Likewise, Adolf Hitler's importance lies not in his appreciation of Wagner or Gothic architecture but in his relentlessly irrational pursuit of race hatred, sacrifice, and war.

When the historical facts are scrutinized by this standard, Columbus's importance becomes clear: Columbus *did* discover America—*for Europe*. Prior to 1492, Europeans lived in total ignorance of the Western hemisphere and the people who inhabited it. Columbus and those who followed him lifted that cover of ignorance—they "dis-covered" America. Once this knowledge had kindled Europe's interest in the New World, European colonists came in growing numbers, bringing with them the wisdom of Western civilization in a vast westward movement, laying the groundwork for mankind's greatest political and economic achievement, the United States of America. Seen in this light, Columbus's voyage is the only one that truly made a difference historically.[4]

Columbus's discovery of America was objectively more important than anything the Indians ever did, from the day the first Indians arrived on the North American continent until the 12th day of October, 1492. No one disputes that some primitive human being, name unknown, at some long forgotten time, somehow became the first person to migrate to the Americas, probably by walking across a natural land bridge from Asia. The only dispute is over the historical significance of that event. In the thousands of years that followed, some Indians showed progress in the application of reason and the division of labor to the problem of existence. But on the other side of the world, European and Asian societies had already passed through those same stages of development. By 1492, Europe had progressed far beyond the American Indians; in the next five centuries, Western

---

4.   Strictly speaking, of course, Columbus never set foot on the North American continent. However, "America" in this context refers not only to North America but to Middle and South America and the nearby Caribbean islands that Columbus did explore, pointing the way for others, such as Giovanni Caboto (John Cabot), another Genoese, who in 1497 explored the northeast coast of North America for England.

civilization would progress further yet, to then-unimagined heights. Columbus brought all of that achievement, actual and potential, with him to the shores of America in 1492. Leif Erickson never did that, nor did any Indian.[5]

The enormous value of Columbus's gift to the Indians should be obvious to all, now if not then. All human beings, of whatever race or ethnic background, should agree that Christopher Columbus's discovery of America is a magnificent event, because it opened up an entire continent to people whose ideas led eventually to the birth of the United States of America. To teach that the Indian settlement of America was of equal or greater importance than the Europeans' settlement is to declare that Indian culture is of equivalent stature to Western culture. But doing something first, chronologically speaking, means little or nothing unless it *leads somewhere.* That is why the discoveries by Indians and Vikings should forever remain as footnotes to the voyages of Columbus.

For this same reason, incidentally, it is entirely appropriate to refer to the aboriginal population as "American Indians" rather than "Native Americans." Columbus called the aborigines "Indians" because he thought he had found islands near China and Japan that were part of the Indies. It was never a pejorative term; it was purely descriptive in a geographical sense. Thus, the name "Indian" stands as an eternal reminder that Columbus, not the Indians themselves, brought the Western hemisphere and its peoples to the attention of Europe. If the Indians themselves had sailed east, landed in Spain, and revealed to Europeans the existence and accurate location of their lands, they would never have been mistaken for "Indians." The

---

5. In this regard, it is significant that one never hears condemnation of the Vikings, or the Chinese, Japanese, Irish, or Welsh, or any other purported pre-Columbian voyagers, for having inaugurated centuries of "ecocide" and genocide. By focusing all their attention on Columbus, his enemies confess their agreement that his voyage was the only one that mattered.

attempt to eradicate the name "Indians" is thus an attempt to obliterate both the memory of Columbus and the relative superiority of the civilization that equipped him to set sail, and the attempt should be opposed for that reason. (Besides, anyone born here is a native; no one ethnic group can arrogate to itself that characteristic.)

Looking at this same point from a different perspective, the Indians, although they perceived the soil of North America, never discovered its true potential. Just as the first Indian who picked up a rock containing uranium did not "discover" uranium, because he did not understand its nature or its potential for atomic power, so the Indians who physically saw and lived on the American lands did not truly "discover" America. It fell to Columbus and the European settlers who followed him to understand and appreciate the full potential of the land and its natural resources.[6]

Finally, there is yet another sense in which Columbus, not the Indians, discovered America. Geographically, the Indians did not understand that the world is a globe containing land masses separated by oceans; their geographical knowledge extended no farther than the relatively short distances they had traveled, on foot or in small boats. By contrast, Columbus and the explorers who followed him showed how the New World related geographically to the rest of the world. In this respect, European explorers and mapmakers allowed the Indians to discover, for the first time, where they had been all along.

---

6. In the minds of rational men, Columbus's name will be forever linked with discovery, as is beautifully illustrated by the following anecdote. On December 2, 1942, scientists working on the top-secret Manhattan project created the first controlled, self-sustaining nuclear chain reaction, in an atomic reactor built in a squash court under the stands of an abandoned football stadium in Chicago. It fell to one of the scientists to telephone government officials with the good news. Wartime secrecy demanded that the true message be disguised, so the scientist announced: "The Italian navigator has landed in the New World. The natives were friendly."

There is only one sense in which it could be said, accurately, that Columbus did *not* discover America. For in truth, he discovered a savage wilderness, not the modern nation that automatically comes to mind when the word "America" is uttered. But by discovering that wilderness, Columbus made our America possible.[7]

Is all this said from the viewpoint of Western civilization? Absolutely. Is that viewpoint something to apologize for? Certainly not. To write history from the Indians' viewpoint would be to concede that their own migration across the Bering strait, many thousands of years ago, was somehow as significant as Columbus's discovery. That would be incorrect; it is improper to teach that Columbus merely "landed in" or "encountered" America, thereby implying that the Indians had already accomplished all the discovering of historical significance.[8]

---

7. This point was made in a letter to the editor of the *Columbus (Ohio) Dispatch* by Thomas J. Meehan, III of Columbus, Ohio.

8. The term "landed in" is appropriate only to describe entry onto a land mass with whose existence everyone is familiar. Thus, Americans did not discover the moon, but they were the first to land men on its surface.

Q

But didn't Columbus and the Europeans who followed him do many evil things to the Indians? What good did Western civilization do for the many Indians who died as a result of the European invasion?

A

All historical actors, Europeans as well as Indians, must be judged in context. That means they should be judged by what was reasonably possible to them, given the intellectual, social, and physical environment in which they lived. For instance, it would be unfair to criticize Paul Revere for having failed to send news of British troop movements via telegraph, because in 1775 the telegraph had yet to be invented. Likewise, it would be unfair to judge Columbus, the Europeans, or the Indians according to standards of moral and political behavior that required five more centuries to formulate and verify.

Western civilization, though pregnant with the possibility of greatness, in Columbus's time had not yet given rise to several of the crucial developments—such as the scientific method, individual rights, and the Industrial Revolution—that later distinguished it historically from all other societies. Indeed, there were several respects in which European culture in 1492 shared some important similarities to that of the Indians.

Philosophically, Europe was still constrained by Catholicism, which was struggling to maintain a series of tenuous, unstable compromises between the afterlife and this world, faith and reason, God's will and natural law, self-sacrifice and self-interest. Thus, for instance, although Columbus understood wind and weather to have natural causes, nevertheless he and his sailors looked to God for deliverance from storms at sea, much as the American Indians might have done in the same situation. Columbus even used scriptural quotations bearing on geographical matters to support his campaign for a western voyage. The idea that God controls the universe, an attitude that permeated the Dark Ages, still held remarkable sway in the minds of Europeans in Columbus's day.

Politically, Catholicism saw no problem with saving souls at the point of a sword; the Western concept of individual rights lay two centuries in the future. Europeans still viewed warfare, conquest, and slavery as normal ways to deal with other men. Between 1450 and 1660, Europe enjoyed only *four years* free of organized warfare. Indeed, during the very same year that Columbus sailed for the New World, Spain defeated and sold into slavery the last Moors in that country while simultaneously ejecting all Jews who refused to accept Christianity. And the notorious Spanish Inquisition, which for the next three centuries tortured its opponents into submission, killing recalcitrant thousands, was reaching its zenith.

Whatever depredations Europeans committed against Indians flowed primarily from these disappearing, yet still important, remnants of Europe's own earlier stages of development. From our point of view, five hundred years later, we would not repeat these same wrongs. But in judging Columbus and those who followed him, we cannot demand omniscience; we cannot demand that they reach forward in time and invent, instantaneously, a natural-law view of the universe, the scientific method, separation of church and state, and individual rights—intellectual achievements that would require centuries of effort by great minds yet to be born. Intellectual discovery, like geographical discovery, is a monumental effort requiring a division of labor over long spans of time. Just as Columbus should not be criticized for having failed to grasp that he had found new lands far from the Indies, so the Europeans should not be criticized for having failed to understand fully the best ways to treat one's fellow man.[9]

Nevertheless, wanton pillaging and acts of unprovoked warfare cannot be condoned in any historical era. The ugly truth is that Columbus and some of his European followers (most especially those who conquered and settled Latin America) forced Christian religion on the Indians, treated them brutally, robbed them, enslaved them, and in a dozen other ways made them more miserable than they already were. But in behaving this way, Europeans treated the Indians no differently than Europeans historically treated each other. And just as importantly, the Europeans treated the Indians at least as well as the *Indians* treated each other. Strong tribes had preyed on weaker ones from the beginning of time, in the West and in the Americas, and slavery was practiced in all cultures before 1492. It was no fluke that many rebellious Indian tribes joined the Conquistadors to defeat the Aztec rulers, who had oppressed neighboring Indians long

---

9. Interestingly, it is always the Europeans who are blamed for not having arrived magically at these truths; no one ever expects the Indians to have understood them. But if Europeans are to be held to a higher standard, the only justification is that they were more advanced than the Indians even in 1492. Thus, to criticize the Europeans and not the Indians is to admit, implicitly, that Indian culture was inferior.

before Columbus's "winged canoes" appeared on the horizon. Finally, it should not be forgotten that the outrages committed by the Conquistadors kindled a flame of sympathy among thoughtful Spaniards such as Bartolomé de las Casas, whose *A Short Account of the Destruction of the Indies* (1552) advanced the then-controversial idea that Indians were fully human and did not deserve to be treated as anything less.

In 1492, no human being—certainly not the Indians—fully understood that natural laws govern the universe; that it is wrong to impose religious beliefs on others; that individuals should be left free of force and the threat of force, so that they may act on their own judgment and thereby build a better world. To discover these facts requires an effort of reason, many such efforts, based on many observations and introspections. In the centuries before the Enlightenment and the Industrial Revolution, people took the mind for granted and assigned it a relatively limited role, the way they assumed that animals would continue to graze and reproduce even if captured and confined. People did not realize that the initiation of force, by preventing people from acting on their judgment, retards the growth of civilization; they felt at liberty to regard other human beings as little better than cattle.

The last decade of the fifteenth century was not a time of great progress on these issues, but neither was it a time of retrogression; everyone was doing just what people had been doing for centuries. But in Western civilization, especially in ancient Greece, lay the seeds of a solution, an answer to the mysteries that had confounded the human spirit for millennia. It was the heirs of the Greek philosophical legacy, men such as John Locke, Thomas Jefferson, and Adam Smith, who showed us a better path, a way to live in peaceful, cooperative, productive co-existence, without religious strife, bloody conquest, and slavery. Their solution was *reason* and *individual rights*, as the civilized alternatives to superstition and force. This was an achievement of Western civilization, unaided by Indian culture.

Nothing in Indian culture came close to providing the seeds of such a radical development.

If Columbus or some other emissary from the West had not arrived in the New World, and the Indians had continued to cling to their pre-rational notions, then Indians would still be enslaving and killing each other today, just as they were doing in 1492. But instead of showing gratitude to Columbus for opening up this hemisphere to the bounty, peace, and freedom of Western civilization, some modern Indian activists still revile all things Western, all things scientific, industrial, and modern, yearning for the day when they can return to the senseless superstitions and oppressive behavior of their ancestors. Such Indians claim a moral superiority they do not deserve.

Q

What excuse was there for taking the Indians' own land, where they had lived for millennia?

A

First of all, it is not correct to speak of the North American Indians as having "owned" the vast expanses of land where they hunted game and gathered food. In order to achieve ownership of previously unowned land, one must first improve it by doing something to make it more valuable than it was in the state of nature. Most North American Indians were nomadic; they moved from place to place, living off wild vegetation and game, never permanently improving the land. In their primitive state, they lacked the capacity to create material values beyond what they could wear or carry, and so their notion of property was likewise primitive: These animal skins are mine, and those are yours. Because by and large they did not permanently improve the land—by enclosing farms, digging mines, building houses with foundations—it never occurred to them that they needed advanced concepts of property. Aside from the spot where

he stood, no Indian could conceive of asserting any lasting dominion over land, certainly not the permanent dominion that Westerners
call ownership.

Private property rights are a condition of ownership; without
them, there can be no crimes against property. People who cannot
grasp the concept of property rights in land cannot lay moral claim
to the protection of such rights. The Indians recognized no universal
moral law that would require one tribe to respect the previous productive efforts of another. Rather, each tribe occupied whatever land
suited its own purposes at the moment, depending on the vagaries of
weather, the game population, and the strength of neighboring tribes.
Tribes that occupied a given place often did so at the expense of
other Indians whom they drove off the land, enslaved, or killed. In
Mexico, the Aztecs engaged in virtually constant warfare, attacking
other tribes and exacting tribute in the form of food, goods, and
bodies for human sacrifice. In North America, the Navajo and Apache
tribes attacked and evicted the southwestern cliff dwellers approxi-
mately 200 years before Columbus sailed west.

Indians held all land collectively, through kinship groups or tribes,
and individuals were accorded no separate property rights. An individual Indian who faithfully tended crops acquired no ownership
rights in them. To this day, the Indian reservations are held collectively by each tribe. "No instance is known of individual ownership
of tribal lands," said a federal court in 1961. The incoming Europeans had every right to abolish such primitive tribal collectivism and
replace it with a system of government based on individual rights, a
government that recognized individual ownership and protected the
values created by individual productive effort, including the rights
of any Indians who were capable of understanding and abiding by
the laws. As the U.S. Commissioner of Indian Affairs said in 1838:

> Unless some system is marked out by which there
> shall be a separate allotment of land to each indi-
> vidual whom the scheme shall entitle to it, you will

look in vain for any general casting off of savagism.
Common property and civilization cannot co-exist.

Because they neither conceived nor acquired ownership rights in
land, Indians had no right to exclude or attack Europeans who sought
to settle there. (On the other hand, Indians like the Pueblos, who
created permanent villages in the Southwest while attaining the highest
level of pre-Columbian cultural development north of Mexico, should
have been allowed to keep and use whatever land they had improved,
so long as they did not pose a threat to civilized settlers.) Moreover,
the vast territories available in North America during the seventeenth,
eighteenth, and much of the nineteenth centuries meant that Indians had access to enough tribal property to support themselves during
the time it took (or in some cases, would have taken) to assimilate
themselves into American society.

The proper approach of a civilized government under such circumstances was described by President Andrew Jackson in his 1829
message to Congress on the removal of eastern tribes to the region
west of the Mississippi River:

> This removal should be voluntary, for it would be as
> cruel as unjust to compel the aborigines to abandon
> the graves of their fathers and seek a home in a dis-
> tant land. But they should be distinctly informed that
> if they remain within the limits of the States they
> must be subject to their laws. In return for their obe-
> dience as individuals they will without doubt be
> protected in the enjoyment of those possessions which
> they have improved by their industry. But it seems
> to me visionary to suppose that in this state of things
> claims can be allowed on tracts of country on which
> they have neither dwelt nor made improvements,
> merely because they have seen them from the moun-
> tain or passed them in the chase.

Today's pro-Indian activists want "reparations," in the form of
valuable parcels of mineral-rich real estate, to be handed over free of

charge to persons of Indian blood, without effort on their part, merely because their great-great-great-great-grandfathers may have chased buffalo or worshiped spirits there. The colossal injustice of such schemes is manifest.

Q

Aren't Europeans to blame for introducing diseases such as small-pox and measles to the New World, killing many Indians?

A

Scientific research has shown that much of the decrease in Indian population during the first decades after the Europeans' arrival was due to diseases of European origin. No one is to blame for the spread of disease in the pre-scientific era. Not even the Europeans had any idea what causes diseases or how they are spread. It was the growth of the scientific method that finally found cures for small-pox, measles, syphilis, and tuberculosis. The emergence of science was an achievement of Western civilization, unassisted by Indian culture.

Today, knowing what we know about the causes of disease, to infect a group of people with a deadly organism would be hideously immoral. But given the European context of knowledge in 1492, it is simply not possible that they intentionally controlled the spread of disease among the Indians. The Europeans are no more to blame for introducing measles and smallpox to the New World than the Indians are to blame for the spread of syphilis, hepatitis, and polio from the New World to Europe.

Incidentally, no one should suppose that the Europeans were spared the ravages of disease on their home continent. The bubonic plague, or Black Death, which killed an estimated one-third the population of Europe between 1348 and 1350, is just one example of how disease in earlier times menaced *all* peoples. Interestingly, however, it was the Europeans' domestication of animals that had the unforeseen effect of rendering Europeans immune to various diseases that later killed many Indians. By bringing themselves into close contact with animals bearing many diseases, large numbers of Europeans sickened and died over the centuries, but others developed immunities, so that finally Europeans achieved widespread immunity. Paradoxically, explains William McNeill, a University of Chicago historian, "the more diseased a community, the less destructive its epidemics become." By dominating the animal world, therefore, Europeans in the long run acquired not only new sources of food and muscle power but also improved immune systems.

All social interaction, especially among persons from different geographical areas, carries with it a risk of transmitting disease. The only alternative would be absurd: to outlaw all travel and social interaction.

Finally, it should be noted that multicultural historians have used faulty analysis to support their assertions that many millions of Indians lived in the Western hemisphere prior to Columbus's arrival and died with the onset of European expansion. The goal of exaggerating pre-Columbian population figures is to support the notion that Europeans were responsible for a genocidal "holocaust" of historical proportions. Although exact censuses were of course never made—even if they could have conceived the idea of a census, the Indians could not have counted high enough—and though reasonable people can disagree as to what are the most accurate figures, the preposterous estimates of 75 million to 100 million aborigines living throughout the hemisphere in 1492, with 8 to 10 million living north of Mexico, cannot be taken seriously.

Q

Didn't Europeans plunder the Indians' wealth, enriching themselves while simultaneously spurring the growth of capitalism?

A

There is no doubt that Europeans who spread through such areas as Mexico and Peru plundered the Indians' precious metals. Cortes and the Conquistadors destroyed the Aztecs' empire, Pizarro the Incas'. The conquerors shipped large quantities of gold and silver back to Spain, enabling that nation to rise to preeminence (temporarily) in Europe.

But it would be a mistake to ascribe too much historical significance to these facts, for the nations that regarded the New World as easy pickings for plunder enjoyed the *least* long-term success in colonization. The Spanish, in particular, acted like gangsters who, having held up a Brink's truck, couldn't wait to spend the loot on guns and fancy clothes. Spain, instead of investing its new-found riches in productive enterprises, engaged in a series of costly wars, culminating in the disastrous attack of the Spanish Armada upon England in 1588. The Spanish also wasted much of the wealth purchased with Aztec gold on useless displays of luxury, at the royal court and in the cities. In short, they knew how to consume but not how to produce. When the treasure finally petered out, the Spanish found themselves a backward nation in charge of faraway lands whose population was demoralized and poor. The Spanish and Portuguese colonies, ever since their heyday, have lagged far behind those settled by northern Europeans.

A point of clarification is in order here. The riches that helped propel Spain to prominence in the sixteenth century did not come from the New World—only the *gold* did. That is, the looted gold was turned into coins and exchanged for valuable goods and services (such as sailing ships, munitions, horses, and skilled labor) available in Europe and other civilized societies. If the civilized nations of the world had not *already* developed a productive capacity far beyond that of primitive tribes, based on centuries of thought and effort and a highly refined division of labor, the Indians' gold would have been nearly worthless. Indeed, it was nearly worthless to the Indians, who used it mostly for ornamentation and were perpetually puzzled as to why the white men were so hungry for it. The Conquistadors, for their part, coveted the gold not for itself but for what they could buy with it, from highly productive, civilized people.

The northern Europeans, by contrast, did not encounter Indian riches, only poor tribes living close to the margin of survival. These predominantly nomadic, stone-age tribes had nothing worth stealing. The difficult task of settling North America was accomplished by Europeans who understood the need for productive work over the long haul. They earned everything they produced. As a consequence of this work ethic, the wealth of the northern colonies continued to grow, generation after generation, long after the plundered wealth of Mexico and Peru had dried up. Here, not in the Spanish speaking colonies, were the seedbeds of capitalism. American schoolchildren still read about the struggles at Jamestown and Plymouth to plant crops so that the fledgling colonies could become self-sustaining. What is less well known is that years and years passed before the Spaniards who settled the Caribbean Islands troubled themselves to till the fertile soil beneath their feet; they preferred to rely on supply ships from Spain until, they hoped, plunder and slave labor would make them rich without working.

So we see that the Spanish, who in key respects represented the most backward elements of a forward-moving civilization, eventually paid the price for their behavior. The *encomienda* system of forced labor that they imposed in Latin America represented, not capitalism, which is based on private property, but a mutant version of feudalism. Although the colonies settled by the Spanish and Portuguese are immeasurably farther advanced today than the Indian cultures they replaced, they still lag far behind the areas settled by northern Europeans. The explanation for these different levels of achievement lies not in race but in culture, not in the ethnicity of the inhabitants but in the ideas they hold. The northern Europeans more fully developed the potential of Western civilization, a potential that was available to all alike, but which was betrayed by many: the potential of reason.

Q

Wouldn't present-day Americans be better off if they could return to the spiritual lifestyle of the Indians, with its slower pace and fewer complications?

A

The spiritual lifestyle of the Indians was anything but relaxed and simple. Indians lived "in a world of anxiety, frustration, inadequacy, and vulnerability, in which the spirits control everything that cannot be explained rationally," writes anthropologist Peter Farb. "Without magic, his life would be one long panic." Because they did not understand natural law, Indians lived in constant fear that fickle gods and spirits might take away the things they depended on for life: plants, animals, rain, even the sun. The Aztecs, for example, believed they were chosen by the gods to feed the sun, which required human blood to fuel its daily race through the sky. So they waged war on neighboring tribes, capturing thousands of prisoners and marching them one by one up to altars built atop massive pyramids. There, in public ceremonies, priests used razor-sharp obsidian knives to slice out their living victims' beating hearts, throwing the organs into braziers where they roasted on glowing coals.

The Aztecs were not unique in this respect, as historian Manuel Salmoral explains:

> Human sacrifice was performed by many of the peoples of pre-Columbian America. Among these were the Nicarao, the Chibcha (who sacrificed children on hilltops), the Tarasco (in honor of the sun), the Zapotec, the Totonac, the Purhua of Ecuador (who poured the blood of the sacrifice down the gullet of a clay idol), the Cañari (who sacrificed 100 children each year to ensure a good corn harvest) and the Chimú (who sacrificed children to their moon deity). The Maya offered human sacrifices in the final stage of their empire, and the Inca resorted to it in times of crisis, such as when they were at war, when there were epidemics, when the Inca emperor was seriously ill and when a new Inca came to the throne.

Nor did all Indians learn the futility of wasting human life in this manner. As recently as *April 22, 1838,* the Pawnees, a midwestern tribe, ritually sacrificed a 14-year-old girl named Haxta, who had been captured from an enemy tribe. Haxta was executed and cut into little pieces, in a particularly grisly ceremony, to obtain fertilizer for a cornfield. The Pawnees then roamed across the farmland carrying pieces of Haxta's still-warm flesh, stopping to squeeze a drop of her blood onto each grain of newly-planted corn.

Torture was not a punishment that the Indians concocted for the white man—torture was an integral part of their lives, a desperate attempt to assert control over an unknowable universe full of intractable spirits. The same savage mentality that led Colorado Indian raiders in 1867 to cut out the tongue of a white captive, stake him to the ground, and build a fire on his chest, dancing and yelling while their victim screamed in agony, also led Haxta's captors to roast her feet over a blazing fire while holding little flaming pieces of wood under her armpits. Indians tortured whites, other Indians, even themselves, not out of hatred so much as fear of the unknown.

The less bloodthirsty Indians practiced their superstitions in the form of hundreds of senseless taboos, such as prohibitions against mixing deer and whale meat, against fishing (because water was a sacred element), even against looking at one's mother-in-law. Such taboos and religious rituals regulated virtually every aspect of the Indians' conduct. Pueblos spent half their waking hours in religious activities. Some tribes practiced so-called "vision quests," in which self-inflicted torture, such as cutting off parts of one's fingers, induced hallucinatory visions of a guardian spirit which they imagined would protect the Indian for the rest of his life.

Many tribes believed that dreams put them in contact with an all-powerful spirit world:

- Members of the Sioux tribe slept with a "dream catcher," a circular hoop with a web made from cow intestines woven over it and a feather dangling from it. The dream catcher, it was believed, would hold captive one's bad dreams, while allowing good dreams to pass through the webbing and slip through the feather, out into the universe to become reality.

- A Huron shaman, in the midst of a deadly epidemic, was instructed in a dream to fast for six days and restore contact with the spirits. The result of his ordeal was the following prescription for his tribe: masked dances, a communion-like rite involving strawberries, and erection of magical scarecrows on village rooftops.

- The Mohawks thought dreams provided premonitions of events which, if undesirable, could be kept from coming true by acting them out in real life. Thus one Mohawk warrior, who had dreamed he was taken captive and tortured by fire, insisted that his fellow villagers bind him and burn him with red hot axes and knives.

In short, Indians had to *feel* out of control because they *were* out of control.

By contrast, modern Americans live in relative serenity due to their understanding and acceptance of natural law. They have no need to trouble themselves that supernatural beings will interfere with their mastery of the environment in the service of their lives. They can confront the natural world with confidence that their efforts to investigate and control nature will meet with success over the long run. The resultant feeling of being "at home" in the universe is an achievement of Western civilization, not Indian culture.

Q

Didn't the Indians live more in harmony with the earth than we do? Haven't the Europeans committed "ecocide" by destroying natural resources and the rich environment that they encountered five hundred years ago?

A

The notion of "ecocide" is a false concept. It is modern Americans, not the primitive Indians, who have established the proper relationship between man and the environment: one of mastery. The Indians, because they never understood the importance of the reasoning mind, natural law, technological progress, and individual freedom, were barely able to scratch the surface of the abundant natural resources available to them. For instance, Indians who lived for centuries atop massive reserves of petroleum needed the European immigrants to show them how oil could be used to light a lamp or run an engine. Likewise, although Aztecs had applied the principle of the wheel to children's toys, Indians continued to carry their meager possessions on their backs or drag them across the ground on long poles. Indians toiled long hours to produce enough food to keep themselves alive; there was usually not enough surplus to permit much division of labor. If Indians produced less garbage, it was only because they produced less wealth. On the other hand, they would think nothing of stampeding a herd of bison over a cliff, taking what they needed and leaving the rest of the dead animals to rot. The Bannock and Northern Shoshone tribes, hunting from horses brought by the Europeans, exterminated the bison that had previously populated the Great Basin.

The environment that the Indians were unable to master, mastered them, as famine, disease, drought, floods, and malnutrition regularly left the survivors helpless and afraid. Describing certain pre-Columbian tribes in his recent history of the American Indians, historian Jake Page writes:

> It was, over the centuries, a hard life. We know from burials that a man of forty-five would be worn down, old; and average life expectancy was less than that. We know that childbearing women suffered more severely from malnutrition than their men (and tended to die earlier), and children more than their mothers. Not infrequently, people died from diseases arising from what we now know to be poor sanitation. Drought came and went . . . .

In most tribes, Indian women were expected to give birth alone, without even the aid of a midwife, and to return to work without delay. Deformed children, twins, and infants whose mothers died in childbirth were often killed or abandoned.

Critics who see in Columbus's voyages the "conquest of paradise" have it exactly backwards, for pre-Columbian America was hellish in its primitiveness.

Modern industrial nations, on the other hand, have truly built paradise, by controlling nature to serve human ends. Applying the accumulated wisdom of Western civilization, America and other industrial countries have achieved ever *increasing* access to supplies of natural resources, including especially energy resources. The materials that make up our environment are not destroyed by economic development; rather, they simply change their form. The human mind, which is an inexhaustible resource, faces the challenge of extracting useful materials and energy from the natural environment as it exists at any point in time. The vibrant economies of the nations adhering to Western values—including, increasingly, the flourishing nations of the Pacific Rim—have banished famine within their borders, attained ever improving standards of living, and created the wealth and leisure necessary for intellectual ferment and the emergence of great art. Natural disasters, though they still occur, are far less deadly and costly due to the protection made possible by modern technology. None of this is due to the efforts of the Indians; all is due to the spread of Western civilization.

Everything that makes life worth living is abundant in the Western nations. Who would trade all that for the life of a pre-Columbian Indian in a pristine environment?

Q

Didn't the Indians contribute to the growth of Western civilization by making it easier in many ways for the Europeans to settle the Americas?

A

In some respects, the Indians made life easier not only for the colonists but also for the Europeans who remained back in their homelands. For example, much attention has been paid to the Indian foods, such as corn, potatoes, tomatoes, and chocolate, that enriched the diets of Europe and the new colonies. Selective breeding of plants by the Indians over centuries yielded better fruits and vegetables than nature had provided them. (Of course, the flow of Old World foods—such as cattle, pigs, chickens, wheat, and sugar cane—to the Americas was just as significant.) European immigrants also benefitted to some extent from the store of geographical and botanical knowledge that Indians had accumulated over the centuries. For example, Indian knowledge of quinine helped Europeans who contracted malaria. To the extent that Indians acted in the service of life, on the premise of hard work and achievement, they deserve our admiration. And to the extent that we benefitted from their efforts, they deserve our gratitude.

But if the Indians had never migrated to the Americas in the first place, had never developed maize or white potatoes or tobacco, had never blazed trails through the hills and mountains, had never built canoes—if the Europeans had encountered continents empty of people—the European colonization of this great land would have occurred anyway. In fact, Europe would have been better off—it could have done everything it did with less human resistance and far less agony. For one thing, the warrior elements of European society would not have been attracted to the stores of precious metals and the prospect of slave labor offered by the Aztecs and Incas, so that more of the Americas—perhaps the entirety of both continents—could have been settled by Northern Europeans, whose better ideas would have led them to make better use of the land than did the Spaniards and Portuguese. This is not a racial truth but a cultural one: Over the span of centuries, northern Europeans chose to apply reason more consistently to more areas of life than did the Spanish and Portuguese, with resultant improvements in moral, political, and economic thinking.

Also, for every benefit obtained from the Indians, there were offsetting problems, primarily the need to deal with warlike tribes. Although not every tribe was equally aggressive, those who did make war on the Europeans impeded their progress in settling North America. Finally, the Europeans had ample intellectual and techno-logical tools to duplicate, in time, everything the Indians had accomplished.

Certainly Europe had nothing of particular value to learn from the Indians' *ways of thinking*—their approach to nature and human relationships, their economies, or their customs. Europeans had already been through their own primitive stages; everything they needed to know, in that sense, they had already learned. By way of analogy, suppose that some modern sailor were to discover, on an uncharted Polynesian island, a previously unknown civilization that had developed agriculture, built pyramids, established religions, and created a calendar. The world would naturally be curious to learn all the details of that society's development. But once anthropologists had written books about that, a rational historian would then ask: So what? What historical significance should be ascribed to that hidden society? The answer would be: little or none. And this would be true *even if that society had been the first in the world,* chronologically speaking, to build a pyramid or design a calendar.

Books have been written listing Indian achievements in many areas of human life. For example, Indians over the centuries improved the potato through breeding. Compared to other crops grown in northern Europe, the potato was a better, more easily grown source of calories. This in turn *contributed to* the growth of Western civilization, because now larger numbers of Europeans could thrive on the same amount of land in Ireland or Germany, and the resulting population growth was important for economic progress. Likewise, Indian mining of precious metals contributed gold and silver from which coins were made. All of these achievements—and many more could be listed—merit our admiration. But the main impetus for the growth of Western civilization came *from within*, not from without. Had the Indians not provided crops and precious metals and the dozens of other materials they supplied, Europe would surely have progressed nonetheless—whether faster or more slowly is a matter for speculation. By the same token, had Western civilization *not* contained within itself such a spectacular capacity for creating wealth and happiness, the potato-eating population would have stagnated in poverty, and the gold would have continued to be made into chalices and decorative masks instead of coins. Abundant natural resources, even when coupled with gradual improvements such as those made by the American Indians, do not generate an Industrial Revolution. For that, it takes *ideas.*

In sum, the Indians were impediments to the best representatives of Western civilization and victims to the worst. Europeans did not need the Indians in order to reach their present level of civilization. The Indians, by contrast, needed Western civilization to lift them up to the modern age.

Q

Surely the Indians are not morally
to blame for the primitive state of
their societies. Were they morally
inferior to the Europeans, who had
gone through the same stages of
primitive society before emerging
into the modern era?

A

Judging the Indians in their context, there is absolutely no reason to blame them morally for the state of their existence in 1492.
To understand the nature of the universe and of man is an enormous
achievement, which required millennia for the Europeans to accomplish. It would be improper to condemn Indians (or Europeans, for
that matter) for living primitive lives in eras when they didn't know
any better. The Indians were not somehow unique because they engaged in the superstitious worship of animals, the horror of human
sacrifice, bloody tribal warfare, slavery, and systematic intimidation
of the individual by the collective. Just look at the history of the

Germanic tribes in Europe, nomadic food-gathering peoples who lived in poverty, engaged in tribal warfare, slavery, and human sacrifice. The simple fact is that every human being now alive had ancestors who lived in primitive conditions.[10] We need not waste our time blaming these peoples for acting in accordance with their severely limited knowledge of man and the universe. We would spend our time more wisely by praising the progenitors of modern civilization who improved upon what they inherited, moving from the relatively primitive to the more rational. For example, Jean Auel's books, beginning with *The Clan of the Cave Bear,* joyously celebrate the individual accomplishments that brought primitive peoples toward the light.

If given enough centuries, the Indians too could have reached an Age of Reason; there is no such thing as racial destiny to dictate otherwise. And it is not as if everything they did was wrong or irrational. But this was a continent of scattered people who had not even figured out how to use the wheel to lighten the burden of human effort. Their implicit philosophy, which was saturated with supernaturalism, irrationality, and collectivism, held them back. Then, suddenly, by virtue of Columbus's voyage, the Indians were confronted with centuries of human progress. For most of the first generation, the task of assimilation was overwhelming (though we

---

10. Though multiculturalists cringe at the mere mention of the concept "savage," especially as applied to the North American Indians, the term's etymology is benign. "Savage" comes from the French *sauvage,* or forest, whereas "civilization" comes from Latin *civilis* and *civis,* denoting towns, cities, and citizenship. Clearly, the emergence of permanent cities is an historical prerequisite for the advancement of human knowledge and industry. By contrast, the concept "savage" denotes that primitive state of society before agriculture and the division of labor have permitted the growth of cities. Only a racist or an historical ignoramus would regard the term "savage," used to describe a person who lived hundreds of years ago, as an insult to, or a threat to the self-esteem of, any living person. The fact is that every person on earth had ancestors who were savages.

have the example of Pocahontas to prove it was not impossible). Then and later, many Indians either ignored the values of Western civilization or, as in the case of the horse and the gun, adapted them to their own violent ends. Inhabitants of the twenty-first century must be very careful not to place unwarranted blame upon primitive peoples who, because of their limited knowledge, could not grasp the tremendous value that was being laid at their feet as a gift from the Europeans.

But all that is in the past. Here we are, five centuries later. Indians have had plenty of time to appreciate the glory of Western civilization. *Now* is when the blame arises, not five hundred years ago. The blame must fall upon those Indians (and their tribesmen in academia and the media) who, living at the dawn of the twenty-first century, still refuse to recognize the superior value of Western civilization, and who call for Indians to abandon their sturdy houses, their pickup trucks, their microwave ovens and their vaccinations, and return to the primitive world of tepees, canoes, campfires, rain dances, and invocations of the spirit world.

Q

Is anyone who points out the faults of Columbus and those who came later an enemy of Western civilization?

A

Merely pointing out the faults of Christopher Columbus does not make one an enemy of Western civilization—if the criticisms are made in context. That is, one who acknowledges the supreme achievement of Western civilization is entitled to point out that Columbus represented a certain stage in the growth of that civilization, which would show much improvement in the future. But a critic who maintains that Western civilization stacks up poorly against *Indian* culture, is at least implicitly asserting that Columbus's role in the spread of Western civilization is to be held against him, not to his credit. This attitude must not be condoned. Those who criticize Columbus and extol Indian culture must explain how they reconcile that position with the celebration of Western culture. If they refuse to acknowledge the objective value of Western civilization, then they are the enemies of Western civilization. There is no middle ground.

That being said, Columbus has been justly criticized for certain failings, most notably his administration of the colonies he founded. After his third voyage, he suffered the ignominy of being returned to Spain clad in chains to answer for his actions. (The cover of this book shows one artist's depiction of Columbus during this time of humiliation.) Yet the deficiencies Columbus exhibited as a governor of men, like the virtues he displayed as a master sailor and intrepid explorer, must be evaluated in the full context of his life in order that historical justice be done.

Christopher Columbus lived 55 years. Born in Genoa, Italy, in 1451, he died in Valladolid, Spain, in 1506, just 750 miles from his birthplace. He was a contemporary of such giants of the Renaissance as Leonardo da Vinci (1452–1519), Nicholas Copernicus (1473–1543), and Michelangelo (1474–1564).

Columbus was named after St. Christopher, the patron saint of travelers, a legendary pagan who is said to have carried baby Jesus across a swollen river. Raised to be a practicing Catholic, Columbus received little or no formal education. Though there is no portrait drawn from life, people who knew him personally described him as taller than average, with a long face featuring an aquiline nose, blue eyes, and red hair.

In his early years, Columbus worked as a wool-comber (his father was a wool weaver), but by his teens he had become a commercial seafarer. Around 1473 he arrived in Portugal, the Cape Canaveral of its day, a launching pad for explorers into the world's vast and uncharted oceans. But at this time, Portugal's efforts were directed at discovering an eastern trade route to the Indies, around the yet-uncharted continent of Africa. Columbus had a different idea. Though the details are lost to history, sometime between 1478 and 1484, Columbus conceived the goal of sailing *west* to the Indies.

Like all great ideas, Columbus's plan did not spring into his mind *ex nihilo* but was the result of many years of experience and preparation. He was an accomplished map maker, a student of maps, and a voracious reader. Prior to his four voyages to the New World, he traveled as a merchant sailor, deck officer, or seaman from Genoa east to the Greek islands; north to England, Ireland, and Iceland; and south to Ghana on the coast of Africa. Thus, before formulating his great plan, Columbus had already sailed to the then-existing eastern, northern, and southern limits of navigation. All that remained for Columbus was to go west.

Beginning about 1485, Columbus sought to convince the monarchs of Spain to fund his effort. During this same period, Portugal, France, and England turned him down. Why did he seek royal favor? Columbus could probably have arranged financing for a private voyage, but he knew that if he was to profit from a successful voyage of discovery he would need the backing of a sovereign who could legitimize his efforts, provide government for newfound lands, and guarantee his safety and status against inevitable challenges by other mariners and their national sponsors.

A special commission met in 1486 to investigate Columbus's plan, but its report—finally issued in 1490—was unfavorable. Ironically, the commission had good reasons to demur, as its estimate of the globe's girth was more accurate than that of Columbus, who had underestimated it significantly. Besides, Spain was reluctant to embark on such a speculative exploratory enterprise until the Moors had been expelled from the Iberian peninsula, a task that was virtually completed by 1492, in which year Columbus finally gained the support of the Spanish monarchs, Isabella and Ferdinand.

Columbus eventually made four voyages to the New World, returning safely every time (though not without mishap). The voyages normally required five to ten weeks in each direction (with variations due to prevailing winds):

- **The First Voyage** (1492–93) (three ships, crew of ninety men): Columbus and his men landed on an island in the

Bahamas, then discovered Hispaniola (now occupied by Haiti and the Dominican Republic), sighted Cuba, explored Puerto Rico, gathered specimens, and seized natives during his three-month stay in the Caribbean. Because one of his ships, the *Santa María,* ran aground and was lost at Hispaniola, and another ship, the *Pinta,* had sailed off to parts unknown, Columbus had only one ship left—the *Niña,* his smallest—and therefore could not consider transporting all his sailors home. Hence, he left thirty-nine volunteers behind to found a colony while he returned in triumph (along with the now-located *Pinta*) to spread the news throughout Europe. He was received as a hero at court and had no trouble persuading those in power to fund a second voyage.

- **The Second Voyage** (1493–96) (seventeen ships and 1,200 colonists): Columbus explored the Lesser Antilles (Dominica), the Leeward Islands, and Puerto Rico. On arriving at the colony in Hispaniola, he discovered that the natives had slaughtered all thirty-nine of the volunteers he had left behind the previous year, probably in response to abuses by the Spaniards. After depositing his new load of colonists, he sailed off to explore Cuba. When he returned, chaos reigned; his subsequent crude attempts to enforce discipline angered the colonists, some of whom returned to Spain, complaining upon their arrival of Columbus's poor administration. After establishing Santo Domingo, which was in a more favorable location than the original colony, Columbus returned to Spain after two and one-half years in the New World.

- **The Third Voyage** (1498–1500) (six ships): Columbus explored Trinidad, sailed across mouth of the Orinoco River, and went ashore in what is now Venezuela (becoming the first European since the Vikings to set foot on an American mainland). Arriving at the Santo Domingo colony, he found the Indians suffering, the colonists in revolt, and syphilis rampant. In 1500, an independent governor arrived, sent by Ferdinand and Isabella based on reports of chaos in the colony, and the governor sent Columbus back to Spain clad in chains after two and one-quarter years abroad.

- **The Fourth Voyage** (1502–04) (four ships): Columbus abandoned the task of governance, for which he was never well suited, and returned to exploration, still hoping to find a route to Cathay. He explored the coast of Central America, including what are now Honduras, Nicaragua, and Panama, never realizing how close he stood (a mere fifty miles away at one point) to the Pacific Ocean, which could have carried him the rest of the way around the world. Shipwrecked in Jamaica, he frightened the natives into supplying food and water by pretending to cause a solar eclipse that his almanac told him was coming. Columbus returned to Spain sick and disappointed, having spent another two and one-quarter years in the New World and having lost all four of his ships.

A word on Columbus's "disgrace" and his removal to Europe in chains after his third voyage: This man was a sailor and explorer, not a governor. He had no training or experience in government, and no knowledge of how to establish and administer a new colony among savage Indians in a distant land (a task that proved daunting to other European powers as well, even centuries later). Who did have such knowledge? *No one.* It is all very well to say, from the vantage point of hindsight, that he should not have sought political power so eagerly. But what was his alternative? The art of colonization had been practiced but little since the Roman Empire disintegrated. There was no established procedure for Spain to extend her dominion over a colony. Indeed, Spain's regional governments were themselves in the process of coalescing into a nation-state after a series of bloody battles that drove the Moors off the Iberian peninsula. To the extent that Spain's monarchs defaulted on their duty to send responsible governors and militia to the New World, to secure whatever lands

Columbus might discover, that was their fault, not his. As Columbus biographer John Dyson put it:

> [T]o hold Columbus accountable for the chain of disasters that followed would be to overlook the essence of the man. He was at bottom a simple seafarer of unusual curiosity, vision and ambition but of indifferent education, questionable leadership qualities and no administrative experience. His power resulted from a single voyage during which many of his shortcomings as a leader were manifest and almost defeated him. Now, setting up a colony in an alien land, he was expected to cope with problems that ranged from town planning and gold mining to civil defense. As well, the majority of his twelve hundred colonists were prickly and headstrong *hidalgos* [members of the lower nobility of Spain]. He was out of his depth. . . .
>
> Columbus evidently had in mind a contented and stable little trading colony on the Genoese pattern, but he found himself in charge of a nursery of conquistadors. Spaniards lived to fight, not engage in commerce or plant crops. Conditioned by their own recent tradition of reconquest, they knew only the doctrine of constant military advance and sharing of spoils. The admiral [Columbus] had led them to believe they would live like lords with docile natives tilling their crops and bringing them fistfuls of gold. Instead they lived in miserable conditions, facing hostile Indians.

Columbus chose a poor location for the colony, then watched in dismay as the loot-hungry conquistadors disintegrated into brutal gangs who terrorized the Indians. Unjustly, Columbus punished the natives, not the colonists. Desperate for an economic return to justify the tremendous investment in ships and men, Columbus saw to it that hundreds of Indians were shipped to Spain as slaves, and those who remained were ordered to supply a certain quantity of gold every three months on pain of death. But gold was simply not to be found in abundance. The initial hoard taken by the Spanish was the product of many years' efforts spent gathering nuggets that washed downstream from the mountains. To generate similar quantities now would have required hard labor by more men than were available. Natives who could not fill the quota were hunted down and captured. Some were hanged (in groups of thirteen, it is said, "in honour of Our Saviour and the twelve Apostles."). Others, having had their hands cut off, were released to return to the back country as living testimony to the futility of resistance. Many committed suicide rather than face life as a slave laborer.

The details are repellent, but one need not endorse such abhorrent tactics in order to celebrate Columbus's true achievement: the geographic discovery of the New World.

To his credit, Columbus wrote letters in 1499 to the authorities in Spain, begging them to send a competent judge and legislator to help him govern. In answer, Spain sent Francisco de Bobadilla as chief justice and royal commissioner. Bobadilla's first view of the Spanish colony Columbus had established, upon sailing into the Santo Domingo harbor in 1500, was dominated by the corpses of seven Spanish rebels swinging from gallows. Bobadilla soon arrested Columbus and ordered him returned to Spain, bound in chains. Though early in the return voyage the ship's captain offered to remove the shackles, Columbus refused—his sense of honor demanded that the royal order must be obeyed until countermanded by the sovereigns, and this could not happen until they arrived back in Spain.

Though Columbus was eventually absolved and freed, he lamented the ordeal:

> They judge me as a governor who had gone to Sicily
> or to a city or town under a regular government,
> where the laws can be observed *in toto* without fear
> of losing all, and I am suffering grave injury. I should
> be judged as a captain who went from Spain to the

Indies to conquer a people numerous and warlike, whose manners and religion are very different from ours.

To do full justice to Columbus, one must consider the caliber of the people on whom he was dependent in carrying out his goals of exploration. He was by no means the worst of them; rather, he was one of the best.

Q

If Columbus hadn't sailed west in 1492, surely someone else would have done it soon enough. Why should we regard Columbus as great when his achievement could have been done by others?

A

First of all, not just anyone could have duplicated Columbus's navigation to the New World; there were only a small number of mariners in that era who combined the skills and dedication needed to complete that voyage. Indeed, the historian Samuel Eliot Morison, an accomplished sailor himself who retraced some of Columbus's routes in writing *Admiral of the Ocean Sea,* declared Columbus to have been "the greatest navigator of his age." So, any one of the mariners who were Columbus's contemporaries—say, Vasco da Gama—who might have accomplished the feat in Columbus's stead would have deserved the same high praise from posterity.

It is interesting to speculate, however, on what the future might have held if Columbus had never sailed. There was no historical inevitability demanding that Europeans be the ones to discover the New World. Portugal had no ambition to discover a western route to the Indies, because its long efforts to find an eastern route around Africa finally met with success when da Gama, in a voyage lasting from 1497 to 1499, sailed to India around the Cape of Good Hope. In the absence of a European thrust to the west, the discovery of America could have fallen to the Ottoman Turks, Muslims whose seafaring skills long antedated those of Europe, and who had developed the astrolabe. Thus, because Columbus did what he did, *when he did it*, an Islamic conquest and colonization of the New World was made less likely.

In the end, the historical fact is that Columbus *did* make his voyage, he *did* discover America, and he *did* change the world. No one else can claim that honor.

There is a little story that, while apocryphal, captures nicely the impudence of those who denigrate Columbus on the grounds that "someone else might have done it." As the story goes, Columbus was being honored at a dinner upon returning to Spain from his first voyage. "Señor Cristobal," said one guest to the Genoese explorer, "even if you had not undertaken this enterprise, we should not have lacked a man who would have made the same discovery that you did, here in our own country of Spain, as it is full of great men clever in cosmography and literature." To this comment, Columbus replied by picking up a hard-boiled egg and challenging the assembled worthies to make it stand on end without the aid of crumbs, salt, or sand. After all had tried and failed, Columbus took the egg and set the end of it down hard on the table, slightly crushing the shell, and upright it stood, to the consternation of all those present.

Wordlessly, Columbus had demonstrated an important truth: Once a deed is done for the first time, everybody knows how to do it. Those who trumpet what another man *might* have done, fail to grant proper respect to the pioneer who showed others the way.

Q

Should the Columbus Day holiday be replaced by "Indigenous Peoples Day," as happened in Berkeley, California?

A

Certainly not. If some Indians persist not only in celebrating Indian culture but in preserving some of its practices, that is their right (so long as the rights of others are respected). There is even some historical value in seeing how primitive people lived. But to establish a national holiday to celebrate it is as outrageous as the recent dedication of a memorial at Little Bighorn Battlefield National Monument in honor of the Indians who slaughtered Custer and his troops in 1876. To replace Columbus Day with "Indigenous Peoples Day" or some similar tribute to primitivism would be a travesty, an insult to all that Columbus brought to America.

The Columbus Day holiday stands as a monument not only to Columbus's geographical discovery but also to his diligence in chronicling and promoting it. Of all the putative "discoverers" now touted for the honor of finding America, only Columbus left us a record of what he did, and when he did it. On October 12, 1492, Columbus discovered America—we know the exact date from his carefully written logs, along with the compass headings that marked his path across the Atlantic. Because Columbus eagerly sought recognition and reward for his efforts, and because he adopted self-promotion and publication as the avenues to that reward, the whole civilized world soon knew of his exploits. As a result, the journey to America was transformed, in a few decades, from a great leap of courage to a prosaic exercise in seamanship. So it is fitting that we pause on the anniversary of the date that changed history, to honor Christopher Columbus, not only for his discovery but for the precision that characterized his whole endeavor. By keeping accurate records from which others could repeat his journey and verify his tale, Columbus showed a great respect for the human mind, a respect that would later characterize the scientific method, one of Western civilization's greatest achievements.

Interestingly, although Columbus Day has been widely celebrated throughout most of our national history, it did not become a federal holiday until 1968.[11] In recent years, protests have soured Columbus Day celebrations in many states, and it is only a matter of time

---

11. The Pledge of Allegiance was written by Francis Bellamy in 1892 to commemorate the four hundredth anniversary of Columbus's discovery of America. The Pledge quickly became a Columbus Day tradition and then a daily classroom ritual in schools across the country. In its original form, the Pledge read: "I pledge allegiance to my Flag and the Republic for which it stands—one nation indivisible—with liberty and justice for all." The American Legion in 1923 suggested that "my Flag" be replaced by "the Flag of the United States of America." Then, in 1954, Congressional conservatives who thought religion the antidote to communism added "under God" to the Pledge. In 2002, the recitation in public schools of this two-word endorsement of religion was properly prohibited by a federal court on First Amendment grounds. *Newdow v. U.S. Congress*, 313 F.3d 495 (9th Cir. 2002), *petition for certiorari filed* April 30, 2003.

before the enemies of Christopher Columbus mount a national campaign to eradicate all official sanction of Columbus by rescinding
the holiday. The shameful absence of widespread public celebration
of the five hundredth anniversary in 1992 revealed all too clearly the
powerlessness of Columbus's admirers, in this country and around
the world. Not only was genuine celebration notably lacking, but
the five hundredth anniversary was characterized by disgraceful displays of contempt for Columbus:

- Street signs for Columbus Avenue in Manhattan were van-
  dalized with red paint to read "Genocide Avenue."
- In Berkeley, California, two performances of an "opera" called
  "Get Lost (Again) Columbus" were scheduled for Columbus
  Day.
- A private school in New York assigned fourth-graders to act
  out a play mocking Columbus as a bewildered fool obsessed
  by gold.

More recently, protesters have used physical intimidation to force
cancellation of the annual Columbus Day parade in at least one city,
Denver, Colorado.

By comparison, the World's Columbian Exposition held in Chicago in 1892 was an unabashed celebration of the spread of Western
civilization and progress to the New World. During that event, President Benjamin Harrison described Columbus as "the pioneer of
progress and enlightenment." Now is the time for pro-Columbus
activists to go on the offensive, not just to preserve the official holiday from oblivion but to restore enthusiasm for it by demonstrating
its true significance.

Q

Wherein lies the greatness of Christopher Columbus? Wasn't he just a sailor who got lost and had the dumb luck to run aground on an unknown shore?

A

A person's historical stature is measured by two essentials: the strength of his character and the importance of his achievements. Virtue by itself is not sufficient; strong character coupled with failure yields the tragic figure of an Amelia Earhart. Columbus had both essentials. The greatness of Columbus lay not in his religious zealotry or his acceptance of slavery; in these matters he behaved with neither more nor less wisdom than his contemporaries. Rather, his greatness sprang from the strength of his character—a strength based on reason, independent judgment, and courage—a strength that led him to persevere for many years in spite of disappointment and to discover a new land in which others could work out the problems from which Europe still suffered, so that five centuries later, achievers of *every* race and religion would have a home.

Four essential clusters of virtue led to Columbus's epochal discovery of America: (1) *reason,* including reliance on observation and natural law in making his own, independent judgments as to the shape and size of the earth and the best means of reaching the Indies by sea; (2) *self-interest,* including a desire to be personally rewarded for pioneering a direct trade route to the Indies; (3) *long-range planning,* including patience and perseverance over the many years needed to convince others to finance the expedition; and (4) *courage,* including the willingness to face starvation and death while reckoning with the unknown expanses of the Atlantic Ocean. Columbus's discovery of America resulted directly from putting these virtues into practice. Without these virtues, neither he nor any other explorer would have made the voyage. Understanding the causal relationships between ideas and virtuous actions makes it possible to do justice, not only to Christopher Columbus, but also to every living person who embraces these same ideas and ways of thinking. We value such people in the present because history proves the power of their ideas in the past.

Meanwhile, those who denigrate Columbus's achievement by stressing his ignorance prove themselves ignorant of the very nature of exploration and discovery.

First of all, Columbus was not "lost" when he arrived at an island in the Caribbean. He knew quite accurately where he was, in relation to his point of embarkation, and he knew how to return home. To imply that he should have known more is to judge Columbus by an impossible standard of omniscience. Geographic discovery is an arduous enterprise that often spans many generations. Each new explorer builds on the knowledge handed down by his predecessors. One man cannot discover everything in an instant, and so Columbus must not be criticized at all for mistakenly believing that he had reached the Far East instead of discovering an altogether new land. Columbus was a pathfinder whose mortality unfortunately kept him from learning the true import of his discovery. We only live so long.

Second, it is true that Columbus was wrong, factually, about the size of the earth and its oceans. Columbus believed, based on the scanty geographical knowledge available to him, that the earth was smaller than we know it to be today. Also, based largely upon the reports of Marco Polo, Columbus believed that Asia stretched much farther across the face of the earth than it does. He therefore concluded that Spanish caravels could reach the Indies from Europe in much less sailing time than would actually have been required. Moreover, Columbus did not guess the existence of previously unknown continents to the west of Europe. Although his discovery thus had an element of "luck" about it, that element adds to the magnitude of his achievement. For luck means, simply, the unforeseen event, the unpredicted fact. All geographic discovery involves good fortune. An explorer who eschewed luck, who traveled safely within the known world, would never discover anything new. The reason that explorers such as Christopher Columbus deserve praise is that *they make good luck possible*, at great risk to themselves. To stumble upon something new, one must first approach near to it. A land-bound peasant, or even a sailor who hewed always to the coastline, would never in a million years have had the "luck" of discovering America. It is the fearless eagerness to *approach the outer edge of the known,* where the unknown lies waiting to be seen, smelled, and touched, that separates the trailblazers from the herd. The rewards are great, but so are the risks. Failure, starvation, drowning, and death might have awaited Columbus there beyond the edge of the known world. But he found land instead—land enough for the world's greatest nation to take root and grow—land enough for the world's finest civilization to show just how much is possible when reason guides men's lives. For having led Europeans to these shores, for having shown mankind the way west, Columbus merits the immortality that only history can confer upon mortal man.

Christopher Columbus *was* a hero. On Columbus Day, therefore, let us celebrate.

INTRODUCTION
TO THE APPENDICES

Before multiculturalism spawned the restrictive speech and conduct codes that have come to be known as "political correctness," all kinds of writers commented freely and frankly on the Indian question and, more generally, on the inferiority of primitive existence compared to life in civilized society. Such commentary has now all but disappeared from the scene. In order that modern readers may have a taste of what they have missed, the following appendices have been retrieved from the dusty shelves to which such opinions have been relegated these many decades.

The chief value of these pieces is to suggest the tone of another era in Western civilization, when the superiority of modern life and the value of progress were taken for granted. If this glance toward the past proves refreshing to those who wish to uphold modern civilization in the future, then so much the better. But beware: These pieces are not a "conservative" plea for a return to bygone times. After all, the reason mankind in the twenty-first century is still confused by Rousseau's ideal of the Noble Savage is that intellectuals and commentators in years past proved unable to defeat the ideas that eventually coalesced into multiculturalism. Some of the reasons for this failure are suggested in the pages that follow. For example, one observes an unfortunate reliance by certain authors on satire and derision, in lieu of the serious analysis required to establish the superior *value* of Western civilization on objective grounds. The one luxury no society can afford is to take its own value for granted.

The selections that follow are not offered as a substitute for modern scholarship. To the extent that anthropologists and historians have developed more accurate information than writers in past centuries possessed, those new findings must of course be integrated with our other knowledge. So, for example, if William Robertson, writing in the eighteenth century, was wrong (in the passage quoted below) about how long it takes for natives wielding stone axes to chop down a tree big enough for a dugout canoe, then his statements must be corrected. But plainly such revisions will affect details only, not the fact that chain saws and bulldozers can fell trees faster than stone axes can, and not the general truth that modern technology is far more powerful than primitive muscle power.

Nor are these writings offered as perfect exemplars of social commentary. Indeed, some are so defective that their more obnoxious passages have been excised, so as not to give blatantly collectivist or racist ideas a new currency they do not deserve. But despite some flaws, these writings hint at the spirit that governed an era when proponents of civilization never thought to conceal their admiration for Christopher Columbus, or to mourn the loss of primitive worlds, or to decry the spread of Western values from the Old World to the New.

THE LIFE AND VOYAGES OF CHRISTOPHER COLUMBUS

By Washington Irving (1828)

Washington Irving (1783–1859), the author of such well-loved tales as "Rip Van Winkle" and "The Legend of Sleepy Hollow," was one of the first American writers to be recognized in Europe as a man of letters. He based his biography of Columbus largely on a variety of documents recently discovered in Spain, where he served as diplomatic attaché to the American embassy in Madrid. For more than a century, Irving's view of Columbus was widely accepted.

It is the object of the following work to relate the deeds and fortunes of the mariner who first had the judgment to divine, and the intrepidity to brave the mysteries of this perilous deep; and who, by his hardy genius, his inflexible constancy, and his heroic courage, brought the ends of the earth into communication with each other. The narrative of his troubled life is the link which connects the history of the old world with that of the new.

* * *

It is impossible not to admire the great constancy of purpose and loftiness of spirit displayed by Columbus, ever since he had conceived the sublime idea of his discovery. More than eighteen years had elapsed since his correspondence with Paulo Toscanelli of Florence, wherein he had announced his design. The greatest part of that time had been consumed in applications at various courts. During that period, what poverty, neglect, ridicule, contumely, and disappointment had he not suffered! Nothing, however, could shake his perseverance, nor make him descend to terms which he considered beneath the dignity of his enterprise. In all his negotiations he forgot his present obscurity; he forgot his present indigence; his ardent imagination realized the magnitude of his contemplated discoveries, and he felt himself negotiating about empire.

*   *   *

[Late September, 1492: on the open sea, headed west]: The situation of Columbus was daily becoming more and more critical. In proportion as he approached the regions where he expected to find land, the impatience of his crews augmented. The favorable signs which increased his confidence, were derided by them as delusive; and there was danger of their rebelling, and obliging him to turn back, when on the point of realizing the object of all his labors. They beheld themselves with dismay still wafted onward, over the boundless wastes of what appeared to them a mere watery desert, surrounding the habitable world. What was to become of them should their provisions fail? Their ships were too weak and defective even for the great voyage they had already made, but if they were still to press forward, adding at every moment to the immense expanse behind them, how should they ever be able to return, having no intervening port where they might victual and refit?

In this way they fed each other's discontents, gathering together in little knots, and fomenting a spirit of mutinous opposition; and when we consider the natural fire of the Spanish temperament and its impatience of control; and that a great part of these men were sailing on compulsion; we cannot wonder that there was imminent danger of their breaking forth into open rebellion and compelling Columbus to turn back. In their secret conferences they exclaimed against him as a desperado, bent, in a mad phantasy, upon doing something extravagant to render himself notorious.

* * *

[October 10, 1492: sixty-eight days at sea, and still no land in sight]:
[W]hen on the evening . . . they beheld the sun go down upon a
shoreless horizon, they broke forth into turbulent clamor. They de-
claimed against this obstinacy in tempting fate by continuing on
into a boundless sea. They insisted upon turning homeward, and
abandoning the voyage as hopeless. Columbus endeavored to pacify
them by gentle words and promises of large rewards; but finding
that they only increased in clamor, he assumed a decided tone. He
told them it was useless to murmur, the expedition had been sent by
the sovereigns to seek the Indies, and, happen what might, he was
determined to persevere, until, by the blessing of God, he should
accomplish the enterprise.

Columbus was now at open defiance with his crew, and his situation became desperate. Fortunately the manifestations of the vicinity
of land were such on the following day as no longer to admit a doubt.
Besides a quantity of fresh weeds, such as grow in rivers, they saw a
green fish of a kind which keeps about rocks; then a branch of thorn
with berries on it, and recently separated from the tree, floated by
them; then they picked up a reed, a small board, and above all, a
staff artificially carved. All gloom and mutiny now gave way to san-
guine expectation; and throughout the day each one was eagerly on
the watch, in hopes of being the first to discover the long-sought-for
land.

* * *

[October 11–12, 1492]: As the evening darkened, Columbus took
his station on the top of the castle or cabin on the high poop of his
vessel, ranging his eye along the dusky horizon, and maintaining an
intense and unremitting watch. About ten o'clock he thought he
beheld a light glimmering at a great distance. . . . They saw it once
or twice afterward in sudden and passing gleams; as if it were a torch
in the bark of a fisherman, rising and sinking with the waves; or in

the hand of some person on shore, borne up and down as he walked from house to house. So transient and uncertain were these gleams that few attached any importance to them; Columbus, however, considered them as certain signs of land, and, moreover, that the land was inhabited.

They continued their course until two in the morning, when a gun from the Pinta gave the joyful signal of land. . . . The land was now clearly seen about two leagues distant, whereupon they took in sail and lay to, waiting impatiently for the dawn. . . .

It is difficult to conceive the feelings of such a man, at such a moment; or the conjectures which must have thronged upon his mind, as to the land before him, covered with darkness. . . . [W]ith his anxious crews, he waited for the night to pass away, wondering whether the morning light would reveal a savage wilderness, or dawn upon spicy groves, and glittering fanes, and gilded cities, and all the splendor of oriental civilization.

* * *

[On Columbus's return to Europe, a storm forced him to seek harbor in Portugal, Spain's arch rival in exploration. The Portuguese king was at first dismayed by Columbus's apparent success, while his courtiers dismissed the tale of discovery as a fraud]: Seeing the king much perturbed in spirit, some even went so far as to propose, as a means of impeding the prosecution of these enterprises, that Columbus should be assassinated; declaring that he deserved death for attempting to deceive and embroil the two nations by his pretended discoveries. It was suggested that his assassination might easily be accomplished without incurring any odium; advantage might be taken of his lofty deportment to pique his pride, provoke him into an altercation, and then dispatch him as if in casual and honorable encounter.

It is difficult to believe that such wicked and dastardly counsel could have been proposed to a monarch so upright as John II., but the fact is asserted by various historians, Portuguese as well as Spanish, and it accords with the perfidious advice formerly given to the monarch in respect to Columbus. . . .

Happily, the king had too much magnanimity to adopt the iniquitous measure proposed. He did justice to the great merit of Columbus, and honored him as a distinguished benefactor of mankind; and he felt it his duty, as a generous prince, to protect all strangers driven by adverse fortune to his ports.

*   *   *

In narrating the story of Columbus, [the author] has detailed many facts hitherto passed over in silence, or vaguely noticed by historians, probably because they might be deemed instances of error or misconduct on the part of Columbus; but he who paints a great man merely in great and heroic traits, though he may produce a fine picture, will never present a faithful portrait. Great men are compounds of great and little qualities. Indeed, much of their greatness arises from their mastery over the imperfections of their nature, and their noblest actions are sometimes struck forth by the collision of their merits and defects. . . .

He was decidedly a visionary, but a visionary of an uncommon and successful kind. The manner in which his ardent, imaginative, and mercurial nature was controlled by a powerful judgment, and directed by an acute sagacity, is the most extraordinary feature in his character. Thus governed, his imagination, instead of exhausting itself in idle flights, lent aid to his judgment, and enabled him to form conclusions at which common minds could never have arrived, nay, which they could not perceive when pointed out.

To his intellectual vision it was given to read the signs of the times, and to trace, in the conjectures and reveries of past ages, the indications of an unknown world; as soothsayers were said to read predictions in the stars, and to foretell events from the visions of the night. "His soul," observes a Spanish writer, "was superior to the age in which he lived. For him was reserved the great enterprise of traversing that sea which had given rise to so many fables, and of deciphering the mystery of his time."

.... What visions of glory would have broken upon his mind could he have known that he had indeed discovered a new continent, equal to the whole of the Old World in magnitude, and separated by two vast oceans from all the earth hitherto known by civilized man! And how would his magnanimous spirit have been consoled, amidst the afflictions of age and the cares of penury, the neglect of a fickle public and the injustice of an ungrateful king, could he have anticipated the splendid empires which were to spread over the beautiful world he had discovered; and the nations, and tongues, and languages which were to fill its lands with his renown, and revere and bless his name to the latest posterity!

THE HISTORY OF AMERICA

By William Robertson (1777)

William Robertson (1721–1793), an historian who was also a promi-
nent figure in the intellectual movement known as the Scottish
Enlightenment, was in the midst of writing his history of America when
the colonies revolted against England. The passages that follow are but
small portions of long essays that he devoted to describing aboriginal life
in North and South America. Robertson's writing will be remarkable to
the modern reader for his willingness to point out the inferiority of
primitive existence when compared to life in civilized society. In contrast
to "politically correct" modern scholars, who regard it as their academic
duty to avoid making such value-judgments, Robertson leaves no doubt
that he is a champion of the Enlightenment, of reason and progress, and
of Western civilization over all forms of primitivism. Allowing for the
possibility that subsequent scholarship may in some respects have modi-
fied or superseded the factual understandings that were current in
Robertson's time, his determination to judge the relative merits of human
societies should be an inspiration to historians. (Robertson's footnotes are
omitted in the excerpts that follow.)

What among polished nations, is called speculative reasoning or
research, is altogether unknown in the rude state of society, and never
becomes the occupation or amusement of the human faculties, until
man be so far improved as to have secured, with certainty, the means
of subsistence, as well as the possession of leisure and tranquillity.
The thoughts and attention of a savage are confined within the small
circle of objects, immediately conducive to his preservation or en-

joyment. Every thing beyond that, escapes his observation, or is perfectly indifferent to him. Like a mere animal, what is before his eyes interests and affects him; what is out of sight, or at a distance, makes little impression.

* * *

Among civilized nations, arithmetic, or the art of numbering, is deemed an essential and elementary science, and in our continent, the invention and use of it reaches back to a period so remote as is beyond the knowledge of history. But among savages, who have no property to estimate, no hoarded treasures to count, no variety of objects or multiplicity of ideas to enumerate, arithmetic is a superfluous and useless art. Accordingly, among some tribes in America it seems to be quite unknown. There are many who cannot reckon farther than three, and have no denomination to distinguish any number above it. Several can proceed as far as ten, others to twenty. When they would convey an idea of any number beyond these, they point to the hair of their head, intimating that it is equal to them, or with wonder declare it to be so great that it cannot be reckoned.

* * *

The North American tribes and the natives of Chili, who inhabit the temperate regions of the two great districts of America, are people of cultivated and enlarged understandings, when viewed in comparison with some of those seated in the islands, or on the banks of the Maragnon and Orinoco [tributaries of the Amazon River]. Their occupations are more various, their system of policy, as well as of war, more complex, their arts more numerous. But, even among them, the intellectual powers are extremely limited in their operations, and unless when turned directly to those objects which interest a savage, are held in no estimation. Both the North Americans and Chilese, when not engaged in some of the functions belonging to a warrior or hunter, loiter away their time in thoughtless indolence, unacquainted with any other subject worthy of their attention, or capable of occupying their minds.

* * *

That women are indebted to the refinements of polished manners for a happy change in their state, is a point which can admit of no doubt. To despise and to degrade the female sex, is the characteristic of the savage state in every part of the globe. Man, proud of excelling in strength and in courage, the chief marks of pre-eminence among rude people, treats woman, as an inferior, with disdain. . . . [Women's] condition is so peculiarly grievous, and their depression so complete, that servitude is a name too mild to describe their wretched state. A wife, among most tribes, is no better than a beast of burden, destined to every office of labour and fatigue. While the men loiter out the day in sloth, or spend it in amusement, the women are condemned to incessant toil.

* * *

In other parts of the globe, man, in his rudest state, appears as lord of the creation, giving law to various tribes of animals, which he has tamed and reduced to subjection. . . . This command over the inferior creatures is one of the noblest prerogatives of man, and among the greatest efforts of his wisdom and power.— Without this, his dominion is incomplete. He is a monarch, who has no subjects; a master, without servants, and must perform every operation by the strength of his own arm. Such was the condition of all the rude nations in America. Their reason was so little improved, or their union so incomplete, that they seem not to have been conscious of their nature, and suffered all the animal creation to retain its liberty, without establishing their own authority over any one species. . . . [The bison] is not of a nature so indocile, but that it might have been trained to be as subservient to man as our cattle. But a savage, in that uncultivated state wherein the Americans were discovered, is the enemy of the other animals not their superior. He wastes and destroys, but knows not how to multiply or govern them.

* * *

All the savage tribes, scattered over the continent and islands, were

totally unacquainted with the metals which their soil produces in
great abundance, if we except some trifling quantity of gold, which
they picked up in the torrents that descended from their mountains,
and formed into ornaments. Their devices to supply this want of the
serviceable metals, were extremely rude and awkward. The most
simple operation was to them an undertaking of immense difficulty
and labour. To fell a tree with no other instruments than hatchets of
stone, was employment for a month. To form a canoe into shape,
and to hollow it, consumed years; and it frequently began to rot
before they were able to finish it. Their operations in agriculture
were equally slow and defective. In a country covered with woods of
the hardest timber, the clearing of a small field destined for culture
required the united efforts of a tribe, and was a work of much time
and great toil.

*   *   *

While hunting is the chief source of subsistence, a vast extent of
territory is requisite for supporting a small number of people. In
proportion as men multiply and unite, the wild animals, on which
they depend for food, diminish or fly at a greater distance from the
haunts of their enemy. The increase of a society in this state is limited by its own nature, and the members of it must either disperse,
like the game which they pursue, or fall upon some better method of
procuring food, than by hunting. Beasts of prey are by nature soli-
tary and unsocial, they go not forth to the chase in herds, but delight
in those recesses of the forest where they can roam and destroy un-
disturbed. A nation of hunters resemble them both in occupation
and in genius. They cannot form into large communities, because it
would be impossible to find subsistence; and they must drive to a
distance every rival who may encroach on those domains, which
they consider as their own. This was the state of all the American
tribes, the numbers in each were inconsiderable, though scattered
over countries of great extent; they were far removed from one another, and engaged in perpetual hostilities or rivalship.

MESSAGE TO CONGRESS
ON INDIAN TRADING HOUSES

From President Thomas Jefferson (1803)

Gentlemen of the Senate and House of Representatives:

As the continuance of the act for establishing trading houses with the Indian tribes will be under the consideration of the Legislature at its present session, I think it my duty to communicate the views which have guided me in the execution of that act . . . .

The Indian tribes residing within the limits of the United States have for a considerable time been growing more and more uneasy at the constant diminution of the territory they occupy, although effected by their own voluntary sales, and the policy has long been gaining strength with them of refusing absolutely all further sale on any conditions . . . . In order peaceably to counteract this policy of theirs and to provide an extension of territory which the rapid increase of our numbers will call for, two measures are deemed expedient. First. To encourage them to abandon hunting, to apply to the raising of stock, to agriculture, and domestic manufacture, and thereby prove to themselves that less land and labor will maintain them in this better than in their former mode of living. The extensive forests necessary in the hunting life will then become useless, and they will see advantage in exchanging them for the means of improving their farms and increasing their domestic comforts. Secondly. To multiply trading houses among them, and place within their reach those things which will contribute more to their domestic comfort than the possession of extensive but uncultivated wilds. Experience and reflection will develop to them the wisdom of exchanging what they can spare and we want for what we can spare and they want. In leading them thus to agriculture, to manufactures, and civilization; in bringing together their and our sentiments, and in preparing them ultimately to participate in the benefits of our Government, I trust and believe we are acting for their greatest good. . . .

JOHNSON AND GRAHAM'S LESSEE V. MCINTOSH

Decision of the U.S. Supreme Court
21 U.S. 543 (1823)

In this Supreme Court case, the plaintiff sought to establish title in land on the basis of a purchase from an Indian tribe. The Court rejected this claim, on the grounds that Indian inhabitants of tribal lands "are to be considered merely as occupants, to be protected, indeed, while in peace, in the possession of their lands, but to be deemed incapable of transferring the absolute title to others." In the process of rendering this decision, the Court summarized the history of European occupation of North America.

[T]he tribes of Indians inhabiting this country were fierce savages, whose occupation was war, and whose subsistence was drawn chiefly from the forest. To leave them in possession of their country, was to leave the country a wilderness; to govern them as a distinct people, was impossible, because they were as brave and as high spirited as they were fierce, and were ready to repel by arms every attempt on their independence.

What was the inevitable consequence of this state of things? The Europeans were under the necessity of either abandoning the country, and relinquishing their pompous claims to it, or of enforcing those claims by the sword, and by the adoption of principles adapted to the condition of a people with whom it was impossible to mix, and who could not be governed as a distinct society, or of remaining in their neighbourhood, and exposing themselves and their families to the perpetual hazard of being massacred.

Frequent and bloody wars, in which the whites were not always the aggressors, unavoidably ensued. European policy, numbers, and skill, prevailed. As the white population advanced, that of the Indians necessarily receded. The country in the immediate neighbourhood of agriculturists became unfit for them. The game fled into thicker and more unbroken forests, and the Indians followed. . . .

THIS COUNTRY OF OURS:
THE STORY OF
THE UNITED STATES

By Henrietta Elizabeth Marshall (1917)

Henrietta Marshall's introduction to her American history textbook took the form of a letter to the young friend named Peggy whose request had inspired the author's labors:

> *Four years have come and gone since first you asked me to write a Story of the United States "lest you should grow up knowing nothing of your own country." I think, however, that you are not yet very grown up, not yet too "proud and great" to read my book. But I hope that you know something already of the history of your own country. For, after all, you know, this is only a play book. It is not a book which you need knit your brows over, or in which you will find pages of facts, or politics, and long strings of dates. But it is a book, I hope, which when you lay it down will make you say, "I'm glad that I was born an American. I'm glad that I can salute the stars and stripes as my flag."*
>
> *Yes, the flag is yours. It is in your keeping and in that of every American boy and girl. It is you who in the next generation must keep it flying still over a people free and brave and true, and never in your lives do aught to dim the shining splendour of its silver stars.*

What follow are excerpts from Chapters 1, 2, 4, and 69 of Marshall's textbook.

[A]fter Leif [Erickson] and his brothers many other Vikings of the North sailed, both from Greenland and from Norway, to the fair western lands. Yet although they sailed there so often these old Norsemen had no idea that they had discovered a vast continent. They thought that Vineland was merely an island, and the discovery of it made no stir in Europe. By degrees too the voyages thither ceased. In days of wild warfare at home the Norsemen forgot the fair western land which Leif had discovered. They heard of it only in minstrel tales, and it came to be for them a sort of fairy-land which had no existence save in a poet's dream.

But now wise men have read these tales with care, and many have come to believe that they are not mere fairy stories. They have come to believe that hundreds of years before Columbus lived the Vikings of the North sailed the western seas and found the land which lay beyond, the land which we now call America.

In those far-off times besides the Vikings of the North other daring sailors sailed the seas. But all their sailings took them eastward. For it was from the east that all the trade and the riches came in those days. To India and to far Cathay sailed the merchant through the Red Sea and the Indian Ocean, to return with a rich and fragrant cargo of silks and spices, pearls and priceless gems.

None thought of sailing westward. For to men of those days the Atlantic Ocean was known as the Outer Sea or the Sea of Darkness. There was nothing to be gained by venturing upon it, much to be dreaded. It was said that huge and horrible sea-dragons lived there, ready to wreck and swallow down any vessel that might venture near. An enormous bird also hovered in the skies waiting to pounce upon vessels and bear them away to some unknown eyrie. Even if any foolhardy adventurers should defy these dangers, and escape the horror of the dragons and the bird, other perils threatened them. For far in the west there lay a bottomless pit of seething fire. That was easy of proof. Did not the face of the setting sun glow with the reflected light as it sank in the west? There would be no hope nor rescue for any ship that should be drawn into that awful pit. Again it was believed that the ocean flowed downhill, and that if a ship sailed down too far it would never be able to get back again. These and many other dangers, said the ignorant people of those days, threatened the rash sailors who should attempt to sail upon the Sea of Darkness. So it was not wonderful that for hundreds of years men contented themselves with the well-known routes which indeed offered adventure enough to satisfy the heart of the most daring.

But as time passed these old trade-routes fell more and more into the hands of Turks and Infidels. Port after port came under their rule, and infidel pirates swarmed in the Indian Ocean and Mediterranean until no Christian vessel was safe. At every step Christian traders found themselves hampered and hindered, and in danger of their lives, and they began to long for another way to the lands of spice and pearls.

Then it was that men turned their thoughts to the dread Sea of Darkness. The less ignorant among them had begun to disbelieve the tales of dragons and fiery pits. The world was round, said wise men. Why then, if that were so, India could be reached by sailing west as well as by sailing east.

Many men now came to this conclusion, among them an Italian sailor named Christopher Columbus. . . .

* * *

So ended the great voyage of Columbus. He had shown the way across the Sea of Darkness; he had proved that all the stories of its monsters and other dangers were false. But even he had no idea of the greatness of his discovery. He never realised that he had shown the way to a new world; he believed to the day of his death that he had indeed found new islands, but that his greatest feat was that of finding a new way to the Old World. Yet now being made a noble, he took for his coat of arms, a group of golden islands in an azure sea, and for motto the words, "To Castile and Leon, Columbus gave a New World."

* * *

In 1506 Columbus died. And it is sad to think that he who, by his great faith and great daring, led the way across the Sea of Darkness, and gave a New World to the Old died in poverty and neglect. The men who had wept for joy at the news of his discovery shed no tear over his grave. He died "unwept, unhonoured and un-sung." Years passed before men recognised what a great man had dwelt among them: years passed before any monument was raised to his memory. But indeed he had scarce need of any, for as has been well said, "The New World is his monument." And every child of the New World must surely honour that monument and seek never to deface it.

* * *

JEFFERSON was twice chosen President. He might, had he wished, have been elected a third time. But like Washington he refused to stand. And as those two great presidents refused to be elected a third time it has become a kind of unwritten law in the United States that no man shall be president longer than eight years.

The next president to be elected was James Madison, who had been Jefferson's secretary and friend. He was a little man always carefully and elegantly dressed. He was kindly natured and learned, and, like Jefferson, he loved peace. He soon, however, found himself and his country at war.

Indian War once more

Ever since the Indians had been defeated by General Wayne they had been at peace. But now they again became restless. It was for the old cause. They saw the white people spreading more and more over their land, they saw themselves being driven further and further from their hunting grounds, and their sleeping hatred of the Pale-faces awoke again.

Tecumseh

And now a great chief rose to power among the Indians. He was called Tecumseh or Shooting Star. He was tall, straight and handsome, a great warrior and splendid speaker.

The Prophet

Tecumseh's desire was to unite all the Indians into one great nation, and drive the Pale-faces out of the land. In this he was joined by his brother Tenskwatawa or the Open Door. He took this name because, he said, he was the Open Door through which all might learn of the Great Spirit. He soon came to be looked upon as a very great Medicine Man and prophet, and is generally called the Prophet.

Much that the Prophet taught to the people was good. He told them that they ought to give up fighting each other, and join together into one nation, that they ought to till the ground and sow corn; and above all that they should have nothing to do with "fire water." "It is not made for you," he said, "but for the white people who alone know how to use it. It is the cause of all the mischief which the Indians suffer."

Indian town of Tippecanoe

The Prophet also told the Indians that they had no right to sell their land, for the Great Spirit had given it to them. And so great was the Prophet's influence that he was able to build a town where the Indians lived peacefully tilling the ground, and where no "fire water" was drunk.

General Harrison's Treaty, 1809

Now about this time General Harrison, the Governor of the Territory of Indiana, wanted more land. So in 1809 he made a treaty with some of the Indians and persuaded them to sign away their lands to him. When Tecumseh heard of it he was very angry. He declared that the treaty was no treaty, and that no land could be given to the white people unless all the tribes agreed to it.

The Governor tried to reason with Tecumseh, but it was of no avail. And as time went on it was more and more plain that the Indians were preparing for war.

Tecumseh's speech

Tecumseh traveled about rousing tribe after tribe. "Let the white race perish," he cried. "They seize our land, they trample on our dead. Back! whence they came upon a trail of blood they must be driven! Back! back into the great water whose accursed waves brought them to our shores! Burn their dwellings! Destroy their stock! Slay their wives and children! To the Redman belongs the country and the Pale-face must never enjoy it. War now! War for ever! War upon the living. War upon the dead. Dig their very corpses from their graves. Our country must give no rest to a white man's bones. All the tribes of the North are dancing in the war dance."

After speeches like these there could be little doubt left that Tecumseh meant to begin a great war as soon as he was ready. And as time went on the settlers began to be more and more anxious, for murders became frequent, horses and cattle were stolen, and there seemed no safety anywhere.

Harrison sends messages to the Indians

The Governor sent messages to the various tribes saying that these murders and thefts must cease, and telling them that if they raised the tomahawk against their white fathers they need expect no mercy.

The Prophet sent back a message of peace. But the outrages still went on, and through friendly Indians the Governor learned that the Prophet was constantly urging the Indians to war.

He marches against them, 1811

So the Governor determined to give him war, and with nearly a thousand men he marched to Tippecanoe, the Prophet's village. Tecumseh was not there at the time, but as the Governor drew near the Prophet sent him a message saying that they meant nothing but peace, and asking for a council next day.

To this General Harrison agreed. But well knowing the treachery of the Indians he would not allow his men to disarm, and they slept that night fully dressed, and with their arms beside them ready for an attack.

The attack

The Governor's fears were well founded. For the day had not yet dawned when suddenly a shot was heard, and a frightful Indian yell broke the stillness.

In a minute every man was on his feet, and none too soon, for the Indians were upon them. There was a desperate fight in the grey light of dawn. The Indians fought more fiercely than ever before, and while the battle raged the Prophet stood on a hill near, chanting a war song, and urging his men on.

Every now and again messengers came to him with news of the battle. And when he was told that his braves were falling fast before the guns of the white men he bade them still fight on.

"The Great Spirit will give us victory," he said; "the Pale-faces will flee."

But the Pale-faces did not flee. And when daylight came they charged the Indians, and scattered them in flight. They fled to the forest, leaving the town deserted. So the Americans burned it, and marched away.

When Tecumseh heard of this battle he was so angry that he seized his brother by the hair of his head and shook him till his teeth rattled. For the Prophet had begun to fight before his plans were complete, and instead of being victorious had been defeated. And Tecumseh felt that now he would never be able to unite all the tribes into one great nation as he had dreamed of doing. The braves too were angry with the Prophet because he had not led them to victory as he had sworn to do. They ceased to believe in him, and after the battle of Tippecanoe the Prophet lost his power over the Indians.

DISCOURSE ON THE ORIGIN
OF INEQUALITY AMONG MEN

By Jean Jacques Rousseau (1754)

Although John Dryden (1631–1700) appears to have originated the phrase "noble savage" in his play, The Conquest of Granada *("When wild in woods the noble savage ran"), the idea was popularized by Jean Jacques Rousseau (1712–78) in the long essay from which the following excerpts are taken. Though the words "noble savage" appear nowhere in Rousseau's text, the phrase neatly captures the theme of Rousseau's work, especially the idea that civilization strips mankind of dignity and nobility.*

Let us begin then by laying facts aside, as they do not affect the question. The investigations we may enter into, in treating this subject, must not be considered as historical truths, but only as mere conditional and hypothetical reasonings, rather calculated to explain the nature of things, than to ascertain their actual origin. . . .

* * *

. . . I shall suppose his conformation to have been at all times what it appears to us at this day; that he always walked on two legs, made use of his hands as we do, directed his looks over all nature, and measured with his eyes the vast expanse of Heaven. . . .

If we strip this being, thus constituted, of all the supernatural gifts he may have received, and all the artificial faculties he can have acquired only by a long process; if we consider him, in a word, just as he must have come from the hands of nature, we behold in him an animal weaker than some, and less agile than others; but, taking him all round, the most advantageously organised of any. I see him satisfying his hunger at the first oak, and slaking his thirst at the first brook; finding his bed at the foot of the tree which afforded him a repast; and, with that, all his wants supplied.

While the earth was left to its natural fertility and covered with immense forests, whose trees were never mutilated by the axe, it would present on every side both sustenance and shelter for every species of animal. Men, dispersed up and down among the rest, would observe and imitate their industry, and thus attain even to the instinct of the beasts, with the advantage that, whereas every species of brutes was confined to one particular instinct, man, who perhaps has not any one peculiar to himself, would appropriate them all, and live upon most of those different foods which other animals shared among themselves; and thus would find his subsistence much more easily than any of the rest.

Accustomed from their infancy to the inclemencies of the weather and the rigour of the seasons, inured to fatigue, and forced, naked and unarmed, to defend themselves and their prey from other ferocious animals, or to escape them by flight, men would acquire a robust and almost unalterable constitution. The children, bringing with them into the world the excellent constitution of their parents, and fortifying it by the very exercises which first produced it, would thus acquire all the vigour of which the human frame is capable. . . .

The body of a savage man being the only instrument he understands, he uses it for various purposes, of which ours, for want of practice, are incapable: for our industry deprives us of that force and agility, which necessity obliges him to acquire. If he had had an axe, would he have been able with his naked arm to break so large a branch from a tree? If he had had a sling, would he have been able to throw a stone with so great velocity? If he had had a ladder, would he have been so nimble in climbing a tree? If he had had a horse, would he have been himself so swift of foot? Give civilised man time to gather all his machines about him, and he will no doubt easily beat the savage; but if you would see a still more unequal contest, set them together naked and unarmed, and you will soon see the advantage of having all our forces constantly at our disposal, of being always prepared for every event, and of carrying one's self, as it were, perpetually whole and entire about one.

*   *   *

Being subject therefore to so few causes of sickness, man, in the state of nature, can have no need of remedies, and still less of physicians: nor is the human race in this respect worse off than other animals, and it is easy to learn from hunters whether they meet with many infirm animals in the course of the chase. It is certain they frequently meet with such as carry the marks of having been considerably wounded, with many that have had bones or even limbs broken, yet have been healed without any other surgical assistance than that of time, or any other regimen than that of their ordinary life. At the same time their cures seem not to have been less perfect, for their not having been tortured by incisions, poisoned with drugs, or wasted by fasting. In short, however useful medicine, properly administered, may be among us, it is certain that, if the savage, when he is sick and left to himself, has nothing to hope but from nature, he has, on the other hand, nothing to fear but from his disease; which renders his situation often preferable to our own.

*   *   *

It is not therefore so great a misfortune to these primitive men, nor so great an obstacle to their preservation, that they go naked, have no dwellings and lack all the superfluities which we think so necessary. If their skins are not covered with hair, they have no need of such covering in warm climates; and, in cold countries, they soon learn to appropriate the skins of the beasts they have overcome. . . . [T]he man who first made himself clothes or a dwelling was furnishing himself with things not at all necessary; for he had till then done without them, and there is no reason why he should not have been able to put up in manhood with the same kind of life as had been his in infancy.

* * *

Hitherto I have considered merely the physical man; let us now take a view of him on his metaphysical and moral side.

I see nothing in any animal but an ingenious machine, to which nature hath given senses to wind itself up, and to guard itself, to a certain degree, against anything that might tend to disorder or destroy it. I perceive exactly the same things in the human machine, with this difference, that in the operations of the brute, nature is the sole agent, whereas man has some share in his own operations, in his character as a free agent. The one chooses and refuses by instinct, the other from an act of free-will: hence the brute cannot deviate from the rule prescribed to it, even when it would be advantageous for it to do so; and, on the contrary, man frequently deviates from such rules to his own prejudice. Thus a pigeon would be starved to death by the side of a dish of the choicest meats, and a cat on a heap of fruit or grain; though it is certain that either might find nourishment in the foods which it thus rejects with disdain, did it think of trying them. Hence it is that dissolute men run into excesses which bring on fevers and death; because the mind depraves the senses, and the will continues to speak when nature is silent.

* * *

[T]here is another very specific quality which distinguishes [men from other animals], and which will admit of no dispute. This is the faculty of self-improvement, which, by the help of circumstances, gradually develops all the rest of our faculties, and is inherent in the species as in the individual: whereas a brute is, at the end of a few months, all he will ever be during his whole life, and his species, at the end of a thousand years, exactly what it was the first year of that thousand. Why is man alone liable to grow into a dotard? Is it not because he returns, in this, to his primitive state; and that, while the brute, which has acquired nothing and has therefore nothing to lose, still retains the force of instinct, man, who loses, by age or accident, all that his perfectibility had enabled him to gain, falls by this means lower than the brutes themselves? It would be melancholy, were we forced to admit that this distinctive and almost unlimited faculty is the source of all human misfortunes; that it is this which, in time, draws man out of his original state, in which he would have spent his days insensibly in peace and innocence; that it is this faculty, which, successively producing in different ages his discoveries and his errors, his vices and his virtues, makes him at length a tyrant both over himself and over nature. It would be shocking to be obliged to regard as a benefactor the man who first suggested to the Oroonoko Indians the use of the boards they apply to the temples of their children, which secure to them some part at least of their imbecility and original happiness.

Savage man, left by nature solely to the direction of instinct, or rather indemnified for what he may lack by faculties capable at first of supplying its place, and afterwards of raising him much above it, must accordingly begin with purely animal functions: thus seeing and feeling must be his first condition, which would be common to him and all other animals. To will, and not to will, to desire and to fear, must be the first, and almost the only operations of his soul, till new circumstances occasion new developments of his faculties.

Whatever moralists may hold, the human understanding is greatly indebted to the passions, which, it is universally allowed, are also much indebted to the understanding. It is by the activity of the passions that our reason is improved; for we desire knowledge only because we wish to enjoy; and it is impossible to conceive any reason why a person who has neither fears nor desires should give himself the trouble of reasoning. The passions, again, originate in our wants, and their progress depends on that of our knowledge; for we cannot desire or fear anything, except from the idea we have of it, or from the simple impulse of nature. Now savage man, being destitute of every species of intelligence, can have no passions save those of the latter kind: his desires never go beyond his physical wants. The only goods he recognises in the universe are food, a female, and sleep: the only evils he fears are pain and hunger. I say pain, and not death: for no animal can know what it is to die; the knowledge of death and its terrors being one of the first acquisitions made by man in departing from an animal state.

* * *

The first man who, having enclosed a piece of ground, bethought himself of saying "This is mine," and found people simple enough to believe him, was the real founder of civil society. From how many crimes, wars and murders, from how many horrors and misfortunes might not any one have saved mankind, by pulling up the stakes, or filling up the ditch, and crying to his fellows, "Beware of listening to this impostor; you are undone if you once forget that the fruits of the earth belong to us all, and the earth itself to nobody."

* * *

Metallurgy and agriculture were the two arts which produced this great revolution. The poets tell us it was gold and silver, but, for the philosophers, it was iron and corn, which first civilised men, and ruined humanity. . . .

* * *

. . . The savage and the civilised man differ so much in the bottom of their hearts and in their inclinations, that what constitutes the supreme happiness of one would reduce the other to despair. The former breathes only peace and liberty; he desires only to live and be free from labour; even the ataraxia of the Stoic falls far short of his profound indifference to every other object. Civilised man, on the other hand, is always moving, sweating, toiling and racking his brains to find still more laborious occupations: he goes on in drudgery to his last moment, and even seeks death to put himself in a position to live, or renounces life to acquire immortality. He pays his court to men in power, whom he hates, and to the wealthy, whom he despises; he stops at nothing to have the honour of serving them; he is not ashamed to value himself on his own meanness and their protection; and, proud of his slavery, he speaks with disdain of those, who have not the honour of sharing it. What a sight would the perplexing and envied labours of a European minister of State present to the eyes of a Caribbean! How many cruel deaths would not this indolent savage prefer to the horrors of such a life, which is seldom even sweetened by the pleasure of doing good! But, for him to see into the motives of all this solicitude, the words power and reputation, would have to bear some meaning in his mind; he would have to know that there are men who set a value on the opinion of the rest of the world; who can be made happy and satisfied with themselves rather on the testimony of other people than on their own. In reality, the source of all these differences is, that the savage lives within himself, while social man lives constantly outside himself, and only knows how to live in the opinion of others, so that he seems to receive the consciousness of his own existence merely from the judgment of others concerning him. . . .

I have endeavoured to trace the origin and progress of inequality, and the institution and abuse of political societies, as far as these are capable of being deduced from the nature of man merely by the light of reason, and independently of those sacred dogmas which give the sanction of divine right to sovereign authority. It follows from this survey that, as there is hardly any inequality in the state of nature, all the inequality which now prevails owes its strength and growth to the development of our faculties and the advance of the human mind, and becomes at last permanent and legitimate by the establishment of property and laws. . . .

LETTER TO ROUSSEAU

By Francois Voltaire (1755)

Francois Marie Arouet de Voltaire (1694–1778), author of Can-
dide, *popularizer of science and philosophy, and a leading figure in the
Enlightenment, met Rousseau in 1745. Ten years later, Rousseau sent
Voltaire a copy of his* Discourse on the Origin of Inequality Among
Men, *soon referred to by many as* The Essay Against Civilization. *Voltaire replied with a long letter, of which only the first paragraph is offered
here.*

I have received, sir, your new book against the human species,
and I thank you for it. You will please people by your manner of
telling them the truth about themselves, but you will not alter them.
The horrors of that human society—from which in our feebleness
and ignorance we expect so many consolations—have never been
painted in more striking colours: no one has ever been so witty as you
are in trying to turn us into brutes: to read your book makes one long
to go on all fours. Since, however, it is now some sixty years since I
gave up the practice, I feel that it is unfortunately impossible for me
to resume it: I leave this natural habit to those more fit for it than are
you and I. Nor can I set sail to discover the aborigines of Canada, in
the first place because my ill-health ties me to the side of the greatest
doctor in Europe, and I should not find the same professional assistance among the Missouris: and secondly because war is going on in
that country, and the example of the civilised nations has made the
barbarians almost as wicked as we are ourselves. I must confine my-
self to being a peaceful savage in the retreat I have chosen—close to
your country, where you yourself should be.

THE NOBLE SAVAGE

By Charles Dickens

Household Words magazine – June 1853

This essay is one of many journalistic pieces published by Charles Dickens (1812–70), the author of such novels as Great Expectations, Oliver Twist, *and* David Copperfield. *A prolific writer who, in addition to his novels, edited and contributed to* Household Words *magazine (1850–59) and* All the Year Round *(1858–70), Dickens was not afraid to embrace unpopular causes, as evidenced by his early and vigorous opposition to slavery. This particular essay—in which Dickens scoffs at Rousseau's popular idea of the Noble Savage whose happiness and virtue were corrupted and destroyed by civilization—is included here because it artfully directs an incredulous scorn toward those who affect a preference for savagery over civilization. Despite its shortcomings (some passages are indefensibly overbroad, in apparent attempts at humorous exaggeration), this essay brings Dickens's legendary powers of observation and description to bear, not so much upon the primitive peoples he mentions but upon their modern patrons, who employ the myth of the Noble Savage to denigrate the value of civilized life. However, like the piece by Mark Twain that follows it, this essay undertakes no explanation of why civilization is objectively superior to the Indian lifestyle. Too much is left to implication, including whether there is an objective standard for judging societies, or whether the question is to be resolved by subjective preferences associated with birthplace, race, or ethnicity.*

To come to the point at once, I beg to say that I have not the least belief in the Noble Savage. I consider him a prodigious nuisance, and an enormous superstition. His calling rum fire-water, and me a pale face, wholly fail to reconcile me to him. I don't care what he calls me. I call him a savage, and I call a savage a something highly desirable to be civilised off the face of the earth. I think a mere gent (which I take to be the lowest form of civilisation) better than a howling, whistling, clucking, stamping, jumping, tearing savage. It is all one to me, whether he sticks a fish-bone through his visage, or bits of trees through the lobes of his ears, or bird's feathers in his head; whether he flattens his hair between two boards, or spreads his nose over the breadth of his face, or drags his lower lip down by great weights, or blackens his teeth, or knocks them out, or paints one cheek red and the other blue, or tattoos himself, or oils himself, or rubs his body with fat, or crimps it with knives. . . .

Yet it is extraordinary to observe how some people will talk about him, as they talk about the good old times; how they will regret his disappearance, in the course of this world's development, from such and such lands where his absence is a blessed relief and an indispensable preparation for the sowing of the very first seeds of any influence that can exalt humanity; how, even with the evidence of himself before them, they will either be determined to believe, or will suffer themselves to be persuaded into believing, that he is something which their five senses tell them he is not.

There was Mr. Catlin,* some few years ago, with his Ojibbeway Indians. Mr. Catlin was an energetic, earnest man, who had lived among more tribes of Indians than I need reckon up here, and who had written a picturesque and glowing book about them. With his party of Indians squatting and spitting on the table before him, or dancing their miserable jigs after their own dreary manner, he called, in all good faith, upon his civilised audience to take notice of their symmetry and grace, their perfect limbs, and the exquisite expression of their pantomime; and his civilised audience, in all good faith, complied and admired. Whereas, as mere animals, they were wretched

---

*   This is George Catlin (1796–1872), author of *Letters and Notes on the Manners, Customs, and Conditions of the North American Indians* (1841).

creatures, very low in the scale and very poorly formed; and as men and women possessing any power of truthful dramatic expression by means of action, they were no better than the chorus at an Italian Opera in England—and would have been worse if such a thing were possible.

Mine are no new views of the noble savage. The greatest writers on natural history found him out long ago. BUFFON* knew what he was, and showed why he is the sulky tyrant that he is to his women, and how it happens (Heaven be praised!) that his race is spare in numbers. For evidence of the quality of his moral nature, pass himself for a moment and refer to his "faithful dog." Has he ever improved a dog, or attached a dog, since his nobility first ran wild in woods, and was brought down (at a very long shot) by POPE?** Or does the animal that is the friend of man, always degenerate in his low society?

It is not the miserable nature of the noble savage that is the new thing; it is the whimpering over him with maudlin admiration, and the affecting to regret him, and the drawing of any comparison of advantage between the blemishes of civilisation and the tenor of his swinish life. There may have been a change now and then in those diseased absurdities, but there is none in him.

Think of the Bushmen. Think of the two men and the two women who have been exhibited about England for some years. Are the majority of persons—who remember the horrid little leader of that party in his festering bundle of hides, with his filth and his antipathy to water, and his straddled legs, and his odious eyes shaded by his brutal hand, and his cry of "Qu-u-u-u-aaa!" (Bosjesman for

---

* Georges Louis Leclerc, Comte de Buffon (1707–1788), author of *Natural History* (1749–1804), a 44-volume compendium.

** Alexander Pope (1688–1744), English poet and satirist. In his Essay on Man, Epistle I, Section III, Pope wrote of the "poor Indian" who seeks in the afterlife a "humbler heaven," asking for "no angel's wing, no seraph's fire," only that "his faithful dog shall bear him company."

something desperately insulting I have no doubt)—conscious of an affectionate yearning towards that noble savage, or is it idiosyncratic in me to abhor, detest, abominate, and abjure him? . . .

There is at present a party of Zulu Kaffirs exhibiting at the St. George's Gallery, Hyde Park Corner, London. These noble savages are represented in a most agreeable manner; they are seen in an elegant theatre, fitted with appropriate scenery of great beauty, and they are described in a very sensible and unpretending lecture, delivered with a modesty which is quite a pattern to all similar exponents. Though extremely ugly, they are much better shaped than such of their predecessors as I have referred to; and they are rather picturesque to the eye, though far from odoriferous to the nose. What a visitor left to his own interpretings and imaginings might suppose these noblemen to be about, when they give vent to that pantomimic expression which is quite settled to be the natural gift of the noble savage, I cannot possibly conceive; for it is so much too luminous for my personal civilisation that it conveys no idea to my mind beyond a general stamping, ramping, and raving, remarkable (as everything in savage life is) for its dire uniformity. But let us—with the interpreter's assistance, of which I for one stand so much in need— see what the noble savage does in Zulu Kaffirland.

The noble savage sets a king to reign over him, to whom he submits his life and limbs without a murmur or question, and whose whole life is passed chin deep in a lake of blood; but who, after killing incessantly, is in his turn killed by his relations and friends, the moment a grey hair appears on his head. . . .

The ceremonies with which he faintly diversifies his life are, of course, of a kindred nature. If he wants a wife he appears before the kennel of the gentleman whom he has selected for his father-in-law, attended by a party of male friends of a very strong flavour, who screech and whistle and stamp an offer of so many cows for the young lady's hand. The chosen father-in-law—also supported by a high-flavoured party of male friends—screeches, whistles, and yells (being seated on the ground, he can't stamp) that there never was such a daughter in the market as his daughter, and that he must have six more cows. The son-in-law and his select circle of backers screech, whistle, stamp, and yell in reply, that they will give three more cows. The father-in-law (an old deluder, overpaid at the beginning) accepts four, and rises to bind the bargain. The whole party, the young lady included, then falling into epileptic convulsions, and screeching, whistling, stamping, and yelling together—and nobody taking any notice of the young lady (whose charms are not to be thought of without a shudder)—the noble savage is considered married, and his friends make demoniacal leaps at him by way of congratulation.

When the noble savage finds himself a little unwell, and mentions the circumstance to his friends, it is immediately perceived that he is under the influence of witchcraft. A learned personage, called an Imyanger or Witch Doctor, is immediately sent for to Nooker the Umtargartie, or smell out the witch. The male inhabitants of the kraal being seated on the ground, the learned doctor, got up like a grizzly bear, appears, and administers a dance of a most terrific nature, during the exhibition of which remedy he incessantly gnashes his teeth, and howls:— "I am the original physician to Nooker the Umtargartie. Yow yow yow! No connexion with any other establishment. Till till till! All other Umtargarties are feigned Umtargarties, Boroo Boroo! but I perceive here a genuine and real Umtargartie, Hoosh Hoosh Hoosh! in whose blood I, the original Imyanger and Nookerer, Blizzerum Boo! will wash these bear's claws of mine. O yow yow yow!" All this time the learned physician is looking out among the attentive faces for some unfortunate man who owes him a cow, or who has given him any small offence, or against whom, without offence, he has conceived a spite. Him he never fails to Nooker as the Umtargartie, and he is instantly killed. In the absence of such an individual, the usual practice is to Nooker the quietest and most gentlemanly person in company. But the nookering is invariably followed on the spot by the butchering.

Some of the noble savages in whom Mr. Catlin was so strongly interested, and the diminution of whose numbers, by rum and small-pox, greatly affected him, had a custom not unlike this, though much more appalling and disgusting in its odious details.

The women being at work in the fields, hoeing the Indian corn, and the noble savage being asleep in the shade, the chief has some-times the condescension to come forth, and lighten the labour by looking at it. On these occasions, he seats himself in his own savage chair, and is attended by his shield-bearer: who holds over his head a shield of cowhide—in shape like an immense mussel shell—fear-fully and wonderfully, after the manner of a theatrical supernumerary. But lest the great man should forget his greatness in the contempla-tion of the humble works of agriculture, there suddenly rushes in a poet, retained for the purpose, called a Praiser. This literary gentle-man wears a leopard's head over his own, and a dress of tigers' tails; he has the appearance of having come express on his hind legs from the Zoological Gardens; and he incontinently strikes up the chief's praises, plunging and tearing all the while. There is a frantic wicked-ness in this brute's manner of worrying the air, and gnashing out, "O what a delightful chief he is! O what a delicious quantity of blood he sheds! O how majestically he laps it up! O how charmingly cruel he is! O how he tears the flesh of his enemies and crunches the bones! O how like the tiger and the leopard and the wolf and the bear he is! O, row row row row, how fond I am of him!" which might tempt the Society of Friends to charge at a hand-gallop into the Swartz-Kop location and exterminate the whole kraal.

When war is afoot among the noble savages—which is always—the chief holds a council to ascertain whether it is the opinion of his brothers and friends in general that the enemy shall be exterminated. On this occasion, after the performance of an Umsebeuza, or war song,—which is exactly like all the other songs,—the chief makes a speech to his brothers and friends, arranged in single file. No par-ticular order is observed during the delivery of this address, but every gentleman who finds himself excited by the subject, instead of crying "Hear, hear!" as is the custom with us, darts from the rank and tramples out the life, or crushes the skull, or mashes the face, or scoops out the eyes, or breaks the limbs, or performs a whirlwind of atrocities on the body, of an imaginary enemy. Several gentlemen becoming thus excited at once, and pounding away without the least regard to the orator, that illustrious person is rather in the position of an orator in an Irish House of Commons. But, several of these scenes of savage life bear a strong generic resemblance to an Irish election, and I think would be extremely well received and understood at Cork. . . .

To conclude as I began. My position is, that if we have anything to learn from the Noble Savage, it is what to avoid. His virtues are a fable; his happiness is a delusion; his nobility, nonsense.

We have no greater justification for being cruel to the miserable object, than for being cruel to a WILLIAM SHAKESPEARE or an ISAAC NEWTON; but he passes away before an immeasurably better and higher power than ever ran wild in any earthly woods, and the world will be all the better when his place knows him no more.

THE NOBLE RED MAN

By Mark Twain (1870)

Samuel Langhorne Clemens (1835–1910), who wrote pseudony-mously as Mark Twain, lived in America at a time when Indians still attacked, tortured, and killed settlers and travelers on the frontier. Like Dickens, Twain used satire to criticize writers such as James Fenimore Cooper, whose romantic vision of the Indians, lampooned here, was con-tradicted by Twain's first-hand knowledge of Indian lifestyles. For obvious reasons, this essay seldom appears in modern collections of his writings.

In books he is tall and tawny, muscular, straight and of kingly presence; he has a beaked nose and an eagle eye.

His hair is glossy, and as black as the raven's wing; out of its massed richness springs a sheaf of brilliant feathers; in his ears and nose are silver ornaments; on his arms and wrists and ankles are broad silver bands and bracelets; his buckskin hunting suit is gal-lantly fringed, and the belt and the moccasins wonderfully flowered with colored beads; and when, rainbowed with his war-paint, he stands at full height, with his crimson blanket wrapped about him, his quiver at his back, his bow and tomahawk projecting upward from his folded arms, and his eagle eye gazing at specks against the far horizon which even the paleface's field-glass could scarcely reach, he is a being to fall down and worship.

His language is intensely figurative. He never speaks of the moon, but always of "the eye of the night;" nor of the wind as the wind, but as "the whisper of the Great Spirit;" and so forth and so on. His

power of condensation is marvelous. In some publications he seldom says anything but "Waugh!" and this, with a page of explanation
by the author, reveals a whole world of thought and wisdom that
before lay concealed in that one little word.

He is noble. He is true and loyal; not even imminent death can
shake his peerless faithfulness. His heart is a well-spring of truth,
and of generous impulses, and of knightly magnanimity. With him,
gratitude is religion; do him a kindness, and at the end of a lifetime
he has not forgotten it. Eat of his bread, or offer him yours, and the
bond of hospitality is sealed—a bond which is forever inviolable with
him.

He loves the dark-eyed daughter of the forest, the dusky maiden
of faultless form and rich attire, the pride of the tribe, the all-beauti-
ful. He talks to her in a low voice, at twilight of his deeds on the
war-path and in the chase, and of the grand achievements of his
ancestors; and she listens with downcast eyes, "while a richer hue
mantles her dusky cheek."

Such is the Noble Red Man in print. But out on the plains and
in the mountains, not being on dress parade, not being gotten up to
see company, he is under no obligation to be other than his natural
self, and therefore:

. . . There is nothing in his eye or his nose that is attractive, and
if there is anything in his hair that—however, that is a feature which
will not bear too close examination . . . He wears no bracelets on his
arms or ankles; his hunting suit is gallantly fringed, but not intentionally; when he does not wear his disgusting rabbit-skin robe, his
hunting suit consists wholly of the half of a horse blanket brought
over in the Pinta or the Mayflower, and frayed out and fringed by
inveterate use. He is not rich enough to possess a belt; he never
owned a moccasin or wore a shoe in his life . . . . Still, when contact
with the white man has given to the Noble Son of the Forest certain
cloudy impressions of civilization, and aspirations after a nobler life,
he presently appears in public with one boot on and one shoe—

shirtless, and wearing ripped and patched and buttonless pants which he holds up with his left hand—his execrable rabbit-skin robe flowing from his shoulder—an old hoop-skirt on, outside of it—a necklace of battered sardine-boxes and oyster-cans reposing on his bare breast—a venerable flint-lock musket in his right hand—a weather-beaten stove-pipe hat on, canted "gallusly" to starboard, and the lid off and hanging by a thread or two . . . .

There is nothing figurative, or moonshiny, or sentimental about his language. It is very simple and unostentatious, and consists of plain, straightforward lies. His "wisdom" conferred upon an idiot would leave that idiot helpless indeed.

. . . With him, gratitude is an unknown emotion; and when one does him a kindness, it is safest to keep the face toward him, lest the reward be an arrow in the back. To accept of a favor from him is to assume a debt which you can never repay to his satisfaction, though you bankrupt yourself trying. To give him a dinner when he is starving, is to precipitate the whole hungry tribe upon your hospitality, for he will go straight and fetch them, men, women, children, and dogs, and these they will huddle patiently around your door, or flatten their noses against your window, day after day, gazing beseechingly upon every mouthful you take, and unconsciously swallowing when you swallow! . . .

And the Noble Son of the Plains becomes a mighty hunter in the due and proper season. That season is the summer, and the prey that a number of the tribes hunt is crickets and grasshoppers! The warriors, old men, women, and children, spread themselves abroad in the plain and drive the hopping creatures before them into a ring of fire. I could describe the feast that then follows, without missing a detail, if I thought the reader would stand it.

All history and honest observation will show that the Red Man is a skulking coward and a windy braggart, who strikes without warning—usually from an ambush or under cover of night, and nearly always bringing a force of about five or six to one against his enemy;

kills helpless women and little children, and massacres the men in their beds; and then brags about it as long as he lives, and his son and his grandson and great-grandson after him glorify it among the "heroic deeds of their ancestors." A regiment of Fenians will fill the whole world with the noise of it when they are getting ready to invade Canada; but when the Red Man declares war, the first intimation his friend the white man whom he supped with at twilight has of it, is when the war-whoop rings in his ears and tomahawk sinks into his brain. . . .

The Noble Red Man seldom goes prating loving foolishness to a splendidly caparisoned blushing maid at twilight. No; he trades a crippled horse, or a damaged musket, or a dog, or a gallon of grasshoppers, and an inefficient old mother for her, and makes her work like an abject slave all the rest of her life to compensate him for the outlay. He never works himself. She builds the habitation, when they use one (it consists in hanging half a dozen rags over the weather side of a sage-brush bush to roost under); gathers and brings home the fuel; takes care of the raw-boned pony when they possess such grandeur; she walks and carries her nursing cubs while he rides. She wears no clothing save the fragrant rabbit-skin robe which her great-grandmother before her wore, and all the "blushing" she does can be removed with soap and a towel, provided it is only four or five weeks old and not caked.

Such is the genuine Noble Aborigine. I did not get him from books, but from personal observation.

COLUMBUS

By Joaquin Miller

Joaquin Miller was the pseudonym of Cincinnatus Heine Miller (1841–1913), a poet of the American West who traveled and worked all over the frontier. He was born, his autobiography says, as his parents crossed the border from Ohio into Indiana: "My cradle was a covered wagon, pointed West."

Behind him lay the gray Azores,
  Behind the Gates of Hercules;
Before him not the ghosts of shores,
  Before him only shoreless seas.
The good mate said: "Now must we pray,
  For lo! the very stars are gone.
Brave Admiral, speak, what shall I say?"
  "Why, say 'sail on! sail on! and on!'"

"My men grow mutinous day by day;
  My men grow ghastly wan and weak."
The stout mate thought of home; a spray
  Of salt wave washed his swarthy cheek.
"What shall I say, brave Admiral, say,
  If we sight naught but seas at dawn?"
"Why, you shall say at break of day,
  'Sail on! sail on! and on!'"

They sailed and sailed, as winds might blow.
　　Until at last the blanched mate said:
"Why, now not even God would know
　　Should I and all my men fall dead.
These very winds forget their way,
　　For God from these dread seas is gone,
Now speak, brave Admiral, speak and say"–
　　He said: "Sail on! sail on! and on!"

They sailed. They sailed. Then spake the mate;
　　"This mad sea shows his teeth to-night.
He curls his lip, he lies in wait,
　　With lifted teeth, as if to bite!
Brave Admiral, say but one good word:
　　What shall we do when hope is gone?"
The words leapt like a leaping sword;
　　"Sail on! sail on! and on!"

Then, pale and worn, he kept his deck,
　　And peered through darkness. Ah, that night
Of all dark nights! And then a speck –
　　A light! A light! A light! A light!
It grew, a starlit flag unfurled!
　　It grew to be Time's burst of dawn.
He gained a world; he gave that world
　　Its grandest lesson: "On! sail on!"

ENDNOTES

Page 2

National Council of Churches of Christ in the USA, Resolution dated May 17, 1990. www.indians.org/welker/faithful.htm

"Teachers urge fairness in study of Columbus voyage," *The Sun* (Baltimore), October 14, 1991, p. C2.

Suzan Shown Harjo, "I Won't Be Celebrating Columbus Day," *Newsweek*, Columbus Special Issue, Fall/Winter 1991, p. 32.

American Indian Movement, Press Release, "Re: Indigenous People's Opposition to Celebration and Glorification of Colonial Pirate Christopher Columbus," October 6, 2000. www.aimovement.org/moipr/columbus-oct00.html

Marlon Brando, quoted in Arthur Schlesinger, Jr., "Was America a Mistake?" *Atlantic Monthly,* September 1992.

Page 3

Jack Weatherford, quoted in Adam Federman, "Columbus Day reconsidered by P.I.P.E. [Proud Indigenous Peoples for Education]," *The Mac Weekly*, October 16, 1997, www.macalester.edu/weekly/archive/1997_10_16/news/n3.html; see also Jack Weatherford, "Examining the Reputation of Christopher Columbus," at www.hartford-hwp.com/Taino/docs/columbus.html

Stephen Greenblatt, quoted in Dinesh D'Souza, "The Crimes of Christopher Columbus," *First Things,* November 1995, p. 5 of internet version: www.firstthings.com/ftissues/ft9511/articles/dsouza.html

City of Berkeley, California, Proclamation of 11th Annual Indigenous Peoples Day, www.ci.berkeley.ca.us/citycouncil/2002citycouncil/packet/092402/ 2002_09_24%20Item%2016.pdf

Page 4

Michael Berliner, "The Value of Western Civilization."

Page 5

Peter Schwartz, "Multicultural Nihilism," In *Ayn Rand, Return of the Primitive: The Anti-Industrial Revolution*, p. 246.

Page 6

Russell Means, "For American To Live, Europe Must Die," speech delivered July, 1980, to Black Hills International Survival Gathering, South Dakota. www.russellmeans.com/speech.html.

Page 8

Ayn Rand, "The Objectivist Ethics," in *The Virtue of Selfishness*, p. 24; *see also* Leonard Peikoff, *Objectivism: The Philosophy of Ayn Rand*, pp. 207–20.

Page 9

Jaime de Angulo, quoted in Robert Moss, "We Are All Related," *Parade*, October 11, 1992, p. 8.

Page 15

Ayn Rand, "Racism," in *The Virtue of Selfishness,* p. 127.

Page 21

Robert Moss, "We Are All Related." *Parade*, 11 October 1992, p. 10.

Page 29

James Trefil, "Phenomena, comment and notes," *Smithsonian*, [date unknown] p. 27.

Page 37

Whitefoot v. United States, 293 F. 2d 658 (Ct. Cl. 1961), p. 662 n.7.

T. Hartley Crawford, *Annual Report of the Commissioner of Indian Affairs*, November 25, 1835, *Documents of United States Indian Policy*, p. 74.

Page 38

Andrew Jackson, "President Jackson on Indian Removal" (1829), *Documents of United States Indian Policy*, p. 48.

Page 41

William McNeill, *Plagues and Peoples*, quoted in *Newsweek*, Columbus Special Issue, Fall/Winter 1991, p. 55.

David E. Stannard, *American Holocaust: The Conquest of the New World*, p. 11; David Henige, "Their Numbers Become Thick: Native American Historical Demography as Expiation," in *The Invented Indian: Cultural Fictions & Government Policies*, pp. 169–91.

Page 46

Peter Farb, *Man's Rise to Civilization as Shown by the Indians of North America from Primeval Times to the Coming of the Industrial State*, pp. 48, 60–61, 89, 187.

Page 47

Manuel Lucena Salmoral, *America 1492: Portrait of a Continent 500 Years Ago*, p. 222.

Page 51

Jake Page, *In the Hands of the Great Spirit: The 20,000-Year History of American Indians*, p. 83.

Page 65

John Dyson, *Columbus: For Gold, God, and Glory*, pp. 188–90.

Page 66

Casas, Bartolomé de las. *A Short Account of the Destruction of the Indies*, p. 15.

Samuel Eliot Morison, *Admiral of the Ocean Sea: A Life of Christopher Columbus*, p. 572.

Page 68

Samuel Eliot Morison, *Admiral of the Ocean Sea: A Life of Christopher Columbus*, p. 670.

Page 72

James Barron, "He's the Explorer/Exploiter You Just Have to Love/Hate," *New York Times*, October 12, 1992, p. B7.

Sam Dillon, "Schools Growing Harsher in Scrutiny of Columbus," *New York Times*, October 12, 1992, p. A1.

Benjamin Harrison, quoted in Arthur Schlesinger, Jr., "Was America a Mistake?" *Atlantic Monthly*, September 1992.

BIBLIOGRAPHY

BAITY, Elizabeth Chesley. *Americans Before Columbus*. New York: Viking, 1951.

BERLINER, Michael. "Man's Best Came with Columbus." *The Intellectual Activist*, September 1992, pp. 9–11.

———. The Value of Western Civilization. Paper read at Columbus Quincentennial Symposium, 11 May 1992, at Santa Clara University Center for Applied Ethics, Santa Clara, California.

BRONOWSKI, Jacob. *The Ascent of Man*. Boston: Little Brown, 1973.

CASAS, Bartolomé de las. *A Short Account of the Destruction of the Indies*. Edited and translated by Nigel Griffin. London: Penguin, 1992.

CIPOLLA, Carlo M. *The Economic History of World Population*. Middlesex: Penguin, 1972.

CLIFTON, James A., ed. *The Invented Indian: Cultural Fictions & Government Policies*. New Brunswick, New Jersey: Transaction, 1990.

DOR-NER, Zvi. *Columbus and the Age of Discovery*. New York: William Morrow, 1991.

DRAKE, Francis S., ed. *The Indian Tribes of the United States: Their History, Antiquities, Customs, Religion, Arts, Language, Traditions, Oral Legends, and Myths*. Philadelphia: J. B. Lippincott, 1884.

D'SOUZA, Dinesh. "The Crimes of Christopher Columbus," *First Things*, November 1995, pp. 26–33.

DYSON, John. *Columbus: For Gold, God, and Glory*. New York: Simon & Schuster, 1991.

EDGERTON, Robert B. *Sick Societies: Challenging the Myth of Primitive Harmony*. New York: Free Press, 1992.

FARB, Peter. *Man's Rise to Civilization as Shown by the Indians of North America from Primeval Times to the Coming of the Industrial State*. New York: E. P. Dutton, 1968.

FUSON, Robert H. *The Log of Christopher Columbus*. Camden, Maine: International Marine Publishing, 1987.

HALLIDAY, Fred. "Columbus: An American Savior." *Penthouse*, October 1992, pp. 84–85.

JOSEPHY, Alvin M., ed. *America in 1492: The World of the Indian Peoples Before the Arrival of Columbus.* New York: Alfred A. Knopf, 1992.

LITVINOFF, Barnet. *Fourteen Ninety Two.* New York: Charles Scribner's Sons, 1991.

MANLEY, Deborah, ed. *The Guinness Book of Records 1492: The World Five Hundred Years Ago.* New York: Facts on File, 1992.

MORISON, Samuel Eliot. *Admiral of the Ocean Sea: A Life of Christopher Columbus.* Boston: Northeastern University Press, 1983.

MOSS, Robert. "Blackrobes and Dreamers: Jesuit Reports on the Shamanic Dream Practices of the Northern Iroquoians." *Shaman's Drum,* Summer 1992.

———. "We Are All Related." *Parade,* 11 October 1992, pp. 8–10.

PAGE, Jake. *In the Hands of the Great Spirit: The 20,000-Year History of American Indians.* New York: Free Press, 2003.

PEIKOFF, Leonard. *Objectivism: The Philosophy of Ayn Rand.* New York: New American Library, 1991.

PEVAR, Stephen L. *The Rights of Indian Tribes: The Basic ACLU Guide to Indian and Tribal Rights.* 2d ed. Carbondale: Southern Illinois University Press, 1992.

PRUCHA, Francis Paul, ed. *Documents of United States Indian Policy.* 2d ed. Lincoln: University of Nebraska Press, 1990.

RAND, Ayn. "Man's Rights." In *The Virtue of Selfishness: A New Concept of Egoism.* New York: Signet, 1964.

———. "The Nature of Government." In *The Virtue of Selfishness: A New Concept of Egoism.* New York: Signet, 1964.

———. "The Objectivist Ethics." In *The Virtue of Selfishness: A New Concept of Egoism.* New York: Signet, 1964.

———. "Racism." In *The Virtue of Selfishness: A New Concept of Egoism.* New York: Signet, 1964.

———. "What Is Capitalism?" In *Capitalism: The Unknown Ideal.* New York: New American Library, 1966.

———. "An Answer by Ayn Rand About Indians." *The Intellectual Activist,* September, 1992, pp. 11–12.

REISMAN, George. *The Government Against the Economy.* Ottawa: Caroline House, 1979.

———. "Education and the Racist Road to Barbarism." *The Intellectual Activist,* 30 April 1990, pp. 4–7.

ROSENBERG, Nathan and Birdzell, L.E., Jr. *How the West Grew Rich.* New York: Basic Books, 1986.

SALE, Kirkpatrick. *The Conquest of Paradise: Christopher Columbus and the Columbian Legacy.* New York: Alfred A. Knopf, 1990.

SALMORAL, Manuel Lucena. *America 1492: Portrait of a Continent 500 Years Ago.* New York: Facts on File, 1990.

SCHLESINGER, Arthur, Jr. "Was America a Mistake? Reflections on the Long History of Efforts to Debunk Columbus and his Discovery." *Atlantic Monthly,* September 1992, pp. 16–30.

SCHWARTZ, Peter. "Multicultural Nihilism." In Ayn Rand, *Return of the Primitive: The Anti-Industrial Revolution.* Edited by Peter Schwartz. New York: Meridian, 1999.

STANNARD, David E. *American Holocaust: The Conquest of the New World.* New York: Oxford, 1992.

TAYLOR, Colin F., ed. *The Native Americans: The Indigenous People of North America.* London: Salamander Books, 1991.

WALDMAN, Carl. *Atlas of the North American Indian.* New York: Facts on File, 1985.

WEATHERFORD, Jack. *Indian Givers: How the Indians of America Transformed the World.* New York: Fawcett Columbine, 1988.

When Worlds Collide: How Columbus's Voyages Transformed Both East and West. Newsweek, Fall/Winter 1991.

WINSOR, Justin. *Christopher Columbus and How He Received and Imparted the Spirit of Discovery.* Boston: Houghton Mifflin, 1892.

WOOD, Michael. *Conquistadors.* Berkeley: University of California Press, 2000.

AFTERWORD

W hen I conceived this project early in 1992, I was motivated to defend Western civilization against attacks by primitivists who glorified the Indian lifestyle. At that time, the enemies of Christopher Columbus were doing their best to discourage the world from celebrating the five hundredth anniversary of his epochal voyage of discovery. Why? Because they hated him for having brought the Western hemisphere to Europe's attention, unleashing cultural forces which, over the next four centuries, marginalized the Indians to make room for a more advanced civilization. I hoped, by providing rational answers to the most frequently heard criticisms of the actors in these historic events, to encourage the world to celebrate Columbus Day with enthusiasm, and for the right reasons.

I did not imagine that, less than a decade later, America would come under physical attack by a much more virulent enemy of Western civilization—militant Islamic fundamentalism. When that movement's terrorist disciples destroyed New York's World Trade Center and attacked the Pentagon in Washington, D.C., they declared war on everything America stands for: reason, science, capitalism, and the pursuit of individual happiness here on earth. What in 1992 was a contentious but civilized debate had become, by 2001, a physical war against key institutions of Western civilization. Thus, it is more urgent now than ever that we identify, understand, and defend the virtues of Western civilization against *all* its enemies, foreign and domestic. I only worry that the spread of religiously motivated terrorism to this hemisphere may render some of the issues treated in these pages almost quaint by comparison.

Thanks to The Paper Tiger, intrepid publisher of Objectivist authors, I am now able to present a revised and updated version of the answers I gave in 1992, along with a potpourri of additional, predominantly "politically incorrect" material from the eighteenth, nineteenth, and early twentieth centuries, penned before America's intellectuals had completely papered over the evidence that pre-Columbian America was something less than a paradise on earth. It is my hope that, in years to come, professional historians will approach these issues with the greater objectivity than has been evident in recent decades, so that amateurs like me can retire from the field.

I am grateful to Dr. Harry Binswanger for several valuable points that he has graciously allowed me to incorporate without attribution. Dr. Binswanger also read the entire manuscript and offered many helpful editorial suggestions, as did Dr. Michael Berliner. Earlier versions of this material were read by Peter Schwartz and Dr. Edwin A. Locke, and I benefitted from their comments, too. Naturally, none of these gentlemen bears any responsibility for errors or omissions in this work, and the expression of gratitude for their comments is not intended to convey their approval or endorsement of the present volume.

If I have done my job right, readers familiar with the work of Ayn Rand (1905–1982) will recognize her thinking in practically every paragraph of my essays. And readers presently unfamiliar with her work will—after consulting the essays listed under her name in the bibliography, as well as her best-selling novels, *The Fountainhead* and *Atlas Shrugged*—see her influence just as clearly. It is fitting that Ayn Rand's spirit should fill these pages, because like Columbus she showed mankind the way to a New World, not of geography but of philosophy. By resolving certain crucial contradictions that threatened the long-term survival of Western philosophy—that is, by objectively demonstrating why reason, individualism, and freedom are the moral and practical alternatives to mysticism, self-sacrifice, and collectivism—Ayn Rand discovered and explored a vast and fertile landscape of the intellect that awaits occupation and settlement by future generations.

In the decades since her death, the legacy of Ayn Rand has been preserved and passed on to a new generation not only by Dr. Leonard Peikoff, author of the leading treatise on her philosophy of Objectivism, but also by the organization that bears her name. Founded in 1985, the Ayn Rand Institute—which I thank for having supported an earlier version of this work by distributing it to campus clubs across the country—has established itself as the clear voice of reason in a culture beset by cacophonous irrationality, and as the single most important institutional agent for positive change in the world today. To the extent that any reader is curious about the further implications of the controversial issues addressed here, there is no better place to start than with the Institute's website: www.aynrand.org. (This is not to say that the Institute endorses this book, only that this author endorses the Institute.)

FINALLY, a toast to the future: May the coming decades witness the flourishing of Western civilization, as its great values are more deeply understood and more zealously defended, while its remaining flaws are acknowledged and cast aside, so that on the six hundredth anniversary of Columbus's voyage in 2092, the entire civilized world can rise as one—in full awareness of why justice demands it—to honor and applaud the brave explorer who sailed west into the sunset, little knowing that his voyage would end in a brilliant new dawn for all mankind.